SKI GAMES

A Fun-Filled Approach to Teaching
Nordic and Alpine Skills

Laurie Gullion

Leisure Press
Champaign, Illinois

Library of Congress Cataloging-in-Publication Data

Gullion, Laurie.
   Ski games : a fun-filled approach to teaching Nordic and Alpine
skills / by Laurie Gullion.
       p. cm.
   Bibliography: p.
   ISBN 0-88011-367-7
   1. Skiing for children--Study and teaching. I. Title.
GV854.32.G85 1990
796.93'083--dc20   89-30437
                                                                       CIP

ISBN: 0-88011-367-7

Developmental Editor: June I. Decker, PhD
Copyeditor: Julie Anderson
Assistant Editor: Robert King
Proofreaders: Laurie McGee and Gregory W. Teague
Production Director: Ernie Noa
Typesetter: Brad Colson
Text Design: Keith Blomberg
Illustrations: Mary Yemma Long, Gretchen Walters
Text Layout: Jayne Clampitt
Cover Design: Jack Davis
Cover Photo: David Stoecklein
Printer: Versa Press

Printed in the United States of America

10 9 8 7 6 5 4 3 2 1

Leisure Press
A Division of Human Kinetics Publishers, Inc.
Box 5076, Champaign, IL 61825-5076
1-800-342-5457
1-800-334-3665 (in Illinois)

To
Bruce
and
Nordic Norm

Contents

vi   Contents

Foreword

This book not only introduces a fresh and fun approach to ski teaching, but it's also fun to read. Laurie Gullion displays her imagination and creativity throughout the book by presenting all sorts of games to teach skiing skills.

Too many of us get locked into teaching styles that avoid games because we are afraid to take chances. The game might not work out, or we feel rushed for time, so we fall into structured and secure routines.

I am sure that many of our teaching styles are downright boring, but not Laurie's. One can't read this book and not see the light—and lighten up we must if we want to keep kids interested in learning new skiing skills.

With her game themes, Laurie identifies all the basic skills and drills for teaching children or adults the sport of skiing. She also introduces methods adaptable to any style of teaching and game themes to match students' psychological and physiological ages and stages of development. As we all know, there are different levels of readiness and receptiveness among any group of students, and Laurie suggests ways to involve everyone in the class at their individual levels.

Also included are ideas on dealing with adolescents and ways to change your style of teaching and planning to meet the needs of that particularly challenging developmental period.

In recent years Laurie and I have shared teaching ideas at Professional Ski Instructors of America clinics in the East. Every time we had a new skill, Laurie had a game to teach it. Sometimes we adults didn't play the game as long or as enthusiastically as children might, but as soon as Laurie noticed that some of us had stopped moving and were analyzing again, she would change the theme . . . and soon we were playing another ski game.

Laurie is a good teacher; she has the qualities I have observed as common to all good teachers. First, she is organized, though this may not always be apparent to a casual observer of the games. Second, she is creative. Third, she is knowledgeable. And, finally, she is enthusiastic. Laurie's text demonstrates all these qualities. It is a much-needed resource that can help teachers and coaches around the world make learning skiing more fun.

I can't imagine running a school program, a Bill Koch League program, or a ski school without having *Ski Games* as a resource. And after reading the book, there's no question that I'll be using more game themes in my teaching and coaching. *Ski Games* is a really fine addition to our ski teaching and coaching library.

Mike Gallagher, Director
Mountain Top Ski School
Chittenden, Vermont

U.S. Olympic Team Member, 1964, 1968, 1972
U.S. Olympic Coach, 1984
U.S. National Team Coach, 1980-86
U.S. Ski Hall of Fame, 1988

Preface

Imagine these activities on skis: ape skating, the Great Laser Wars, elbow tag, slow motion follow the leader, slalom races, ski soccer, "blind" skiing with a "seeing eye." These graphic names suggest colorful action and intense involvement in a sport as accessible as the backyard. We can hear the laughter, see children rolling in the snow, and watch them glide magically on their skis.

Gone are the days of lining up children, demonstrating a specific technique, and putting them "on stage" as they practice. Enter the era of learning by doing—lots of doing—in a carefree, noncompetitive arena.

Playing games with skiing was my salvation when as an instructor I was faced with hour after hour of visiting school groups. The traditional approach of teaching a mastered technique just didn't work with kids. Who cared about a good-looking diagonal stride or a perfect parallel turn? These kids had different goals. They wanted to climb the highest hill, race each other on the nastiest downhill, and attempt aerial acrobatics. Forget this technical stuff; building a ski jump was more exciting! To insure that they had a basic understanding (like an ability to avoid obstacles and to stop safely), I introduced games and activities that sneakily taught them the fundamentals of skiing.

They had a great time sliding on one ski, creating ski ballets, skiing with partners, and tumbling and hollering with the slightest provocation. So did I; I was the big kid wallowing in the snow along with the little ones. These miniature bombardiers learned solid skills through playing, and they demonstrated advanced technique without even thinking about it.

Because kids love to play games, their ability to learn new skills through lighthearted play is immense! They stay loose, physically and emotionally. Their curiosity and enthusiasm help the process, but perhaps their willingness to try anything (and risk failure) encourages such quick and effective learning.

Thinking is a big problem in learning. Too many adults begin to intellectualize a sport, and they turn into wooden soldiers. But even adults liked the lighter approach. Parents and teachers joined the children in the games and discovered that their skiing skills increased greatly. They just needed more encouragement—almost permission—to have fun. After all, one just can't have fun without realizing some other benefits!

My fun-loving spirit was contagious, I think, and these new skiers enjoyed themselves. They enjoyed each other. They left the program with solid skills and plenty of ideas for noncompetitive activities that they could share with family and friends. Best of all, they wanted more of it.

The innovative, lighthearted activities in this book are the result of that demand. They provide an up-to-date resource that reflects enormous changes in the way we teach Nordic and Alpine skiing. This book promotes an energetic, enthusiastic approach that provides leaders with an effective alternative.

In this book skills come first—an approach adopted by many ski instructors in recent years. Children enjoy greater success by beginning with basic skiing skills (like balance) rather than immediately confronting the more complex maneuvers (like turns). Gliding on one leg, transferring weight from ski to ski, and skidding on skis are fundamental skills that, among others, lead to improved performance of skiing techniques.

This book provides parents, recreation leaders, and instructors with enjoyable exercises and games to teach skiing. The approach is a simple, descriptive one that provides leaders with a supplement to standard instructional texts. Eight skills and more than 20 maneuvers for Alpine and Nordic skiing are explained simply and colorfully and are followed by lists of activities for practice. A chapter on ski games for larger groups is a handy resource for activities at ski festivals, club outings, or perhaps neighborhood gatherings. Also included are guidelines for organizing safe play.

These activities have been used by ski instructors who needed an alternative to traditional methods of learning to ski, who wanted to expand their bag of tricks. These are instructors who wanted to lead a wide variety of activities rather than the same old thing and wanted their students to be captivated by the sport. They can help you to accomplish the same goals.

Use the activities as a means to excite your children, students, or club members about winter skiing fun. They are a good place to begin and are intended to trigger other creative ideas for play. Modify them to suit the needs of various skiers—from preschoolers to adolescents, from aspiring racers to the physically handicapped. Let them lead you to more new games. The only limit is your imagination.

Acknowledgments

I'd like to thank the following people for their contributions to *Ski Games:*

Trish McCarthy, Outdoor Recreation Program Director at Northfield Mountain Cross Country Ski Area, for her creativity, humor, and inspiration, embodied in her new program ideas for outdoor education.

The ski instructors at Northfield Mountain for creating a wonderful ski playground and sharing successful games.

Bill Gabriel, Ski School Director at Northfield Mountain Cross Country Ski Area and PSIA-E Nordic Examiner, for editing the manuscript, commenting on Nordic skiing, and especially for the humorous scribbles in the margins.

Marty Harrison, Ski School Director at Okemo Mountain, member of PSIA-E Children's Committee and chairman of the PSIA's National Children's Committee, for advice and comments on Alpine Skiing—especially the similarities and dissimilarities between Alpine and Nordic skiing.

Maggie Sjostrom, Children's Program Director at Wildcat Mountain and member of the PSIA-E Children's Committee, for her advice and comments on Alpine skiing and her willingness to share information from PSIA's *Teaching Guide for Children's Instructors.*

John Tidd, former PSIA National Nordic Demonstration Team member and owner of Tidd Tech, for editing the manuscript and commenting on Nordic skiing, and for offering unflagging encouragement from the book's conception.

The Northfield Mountain Recreation and Environmental Complex for office support as well as the opportunity to conduct photo sessions with ski instructors.

Students at the Linden Hill School in Northfield, Massachusetts, who posed for photographs used as the basis for illustrations in the book.

The many games leaders from foundations, recreational organizations, and educational programs who support the cooperative games movement and have contributed to a melting pot of activities. Games in this book are often adaptations of their creations.

The ski instructors, Bill Koch League coaches, and parents throughout the East—too numerous to name—who shared ideas during workshops and contributed to the lists of activities.

The following ski areas for photographs: Killington, Mt. Snow, Northfield Mountain, and Smugglers Notch.

1 A Playful Approach to Skiing

I have great respect for young skiers, and I'm envious, too! Watching their relaxed, supple skiing style is fascinating, and seeing their willingness to experiment is inspirational. Children respond enthusiastically to the challenge of a variety of tasks—especially the unusual ones— and their experimentation leads to enormous improvements in their skiing ability. As adults, we can learn a great deal from their approach.

Playing games with skiing appeals to the natural curiosity and creativity of children. Lighthearted play fulfills their needs to have fun, to be constantly active, and to explore new territory. Give children an appealing challenge, and they leap at the chance to meet it—often literally!

Skiing is just another playground where children can expand their horizons. They see the world as filled with possibilities rather than limitations. They imagine themselves skiing perfectly, and they re-create that image with their bodies. The younger the children, the more fascinating their receptivity to immersing themselves in ski play.

I once stood at the lip of an expert trail with an assured 6-year-old skier who taught me a lesson about confidence. We were choosing a route at Mad River Glen in Vermont, and I asked the boy and his father which trails would be appropriate for the child's abilities. One of the older New England ski areas, Mad River is well known for its steep terrain, natural snow conditions, and "tree" skiing.

We faced moguls, chutes, ledges, and glades of trees that required quick decision making and a variety of skiing techniques. And courage, I thought. But our young leader gave a gentler trail scarcely a glance, chose a particularly torturous route, and descended more smoothly than his adult companions.

This child "skied smart" and effectively by choosing the right moves in the right places. He made me wish for the clearheadedness of a child whose need dictates function. He showed great versatility in executing quick, short turns or longer traverses; in dampening his speed or letting it build; in moving without pause from route finding in the moguls to the trees to the chutes. His approach of never looking back but always looking ahead to the next unknown route infused me with great excitement. We explored as many different trails as possible that afternoon.

A look at this boy's development is revealing. Just past the toddling stage, he had worn his pint-size cross-country skis in the house and on the lawn for the sheer fun of it. Who needs snow when a child has understanding parents?! Balancing and stomping around on skis was a pleasant activity for as long or as short as he wanted. Performing the same moves on snow occurred naturally, and as he grew older, he sought new challenges: more speed, more tricks, more terrain.

He could handle it, because he had solid skills that enabled him to ski safely and enjoyably. I remembered his stories about playing in terrain gardens at the local alpine ski area, where these sculpted obstacle courses offered an intriguing opportunity to practice. He didn't know it, but the gardens established challenging tasks that forced him to develop basic skills (Figure 1.1).

Figure 1.1. Outdoor obstacle course.

Such a playful approach is a natural means to an end. Play enables skiers to practice fundamental skills in a relaxed fashion, and this physical and emotional looseness allows a speedy, efficient learning of new skills. The desire to achieve a particular goal in play motivates a skier to combine skills into specific techniques.

The First Few Steps

The turning point in my teaching came with a group of special needs students who were learning to cross-country ski. Surprisingly, the weather in southern New England worked in our favor. There wasn't enough snow on the first day of the program, so we decided to begin indoors—on rugs! The decision was a good one.

Members of our group had mental and physical handicaps that affected their athletic activities, and balancing on skis was a real issue for them. We took the first tentative ski steps on rugs that offered great traction. No one cared about gliding yet! Standing up on skinny, wobbly skis was a more immediate concern.

Given our limited space, we set up a simple obstacle course with which the skiers moved around chairs and tables in follow-the-leader fashion. The exercise provided practice in all the basic moves—stepping forward, backward, and sideways and turning around corners—without the fear of sliding and falling (Figure 1.2). Our indoor course provided excellent traction! In fact, we named the program Stop! Action! Traction! and created plays such as "freeze" plays and "squeeze" plays. The rules bore a striking resemblance to Red Light, Green Light.

The skiers loved the game because it allowed them to succeed in and enjoy a new activity in a nonthreatening environment. They experienced a wonderful introduction to a program that could have been a dismal failure. When the snow finally arrived, the group members clamored for their favorite game during that first session and in every lesson throughout the season.

In subsequent sessions, we introduced one variable at a time—first walking on skis, then the more unsettling sensation of sliding on skis. It was apparent that one boy with particularly poor balance would have a difficult time descending even a gentle hill.

How could I help the boy negotiate hills safely—with control and without exhausting himself? How could he continue to enjoy the sport with his friends? Every cross-country tour requires a skier to handle varied terrain, and the hills would be a difficult obstacle for this skier.

In desperation, I launched a series of fun, slightly ludicrous exercises on the hill for everyone to practice. I never mentioned my hidden goal

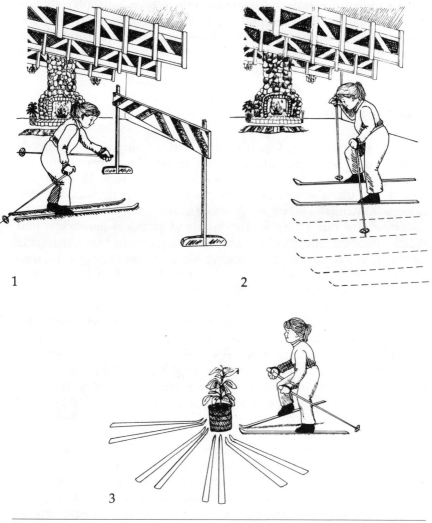

Figure 1.2. Indoor obstacle course.

of safe skill development for the one boy in particular. Instead, I encouraged the skiers to have fun in a crazy way, and we spent what we called a Day at the Races.

The task (which I demonstrated to the group's enjoyment) was to kneel on the skis, hold onto the ski tips like steering a sled, and slide down the hill. Different people excitedly suggested variations on our racetrack theme. We practiced being different types of horses, such as thoroughbreds who toss their heads, rodeo animals who threaten to buck, those who balk halfway down the hill. When everyone had mastered the ability to steer and stop, we held mass races from the top. We had head-to-head competitions and slalom courses. The heavier skiers who stayed on their skis were thrilled to win for a change (Figure 1.3).

Figure 1.3. Day at the Races.

This exercise encouraged safe, controlled sliding on skis and the ability to stop when necessary by tipping over sideways into the hill. The exercise eliminated the fear of a major wipe-out and helped everyone obtain a real feel for gliding and speed control. Most importantly, it helped the group's weakest skier find a method that suited his abilities. The techniques the boy developed may not have been technically correct, but they enabled him to ski safely with his friends.

When the other participants progressed to standing and sliding on their skis, the boy with the poor balance experimented with sitting on the back of his skis and stopping his speed by sliding his buttocks to one side. Later, he happily returned to the Day at the Races exercises and practiced slalom maneuvers on his own. A chaperone told me that the boy joined all the group's ski tours that winter and descended the steep hills in his on-the-knees "race" position. He finally stood on a few, gentler hills. The approach may have been unorthodox, but it worked.

Why shouldn't this approach work with any skiers with poor balance? Perhaps a departure from the traditional lesson plan might help those skiers who are obviously fearful of hills and are too tense to glide successfully on their skis. After achieving success with this method I began to experiment with other unorthodox, nonthreatening exercises as a means of meeting the needs of more skiers.

The Advantages of Play

The beauty of a games-oriented approach is its relevance for all ages and abilities. It encourages intense involvement and practice in all skiers from beginners to racers, children to senior citizens, and abled to disabled. Because of the proven effectiveness of play in teaching skills, Hank Lange, former U.S. Marathon Ski Team coach, often uses his version of a Day at the Races as a warm-up drill when he begins his racing clinics for high school skiers.

Lange leads the group through a series of racing scenarios in which he demonstrates and the group mimics his actions. The action occurs in a small 5-foot area surrounding each skier. Lange creates an imaginary world as skiers follow his directions, and he often describes a typical race scene that might unfold like this:

''We're at the starting line—a mass start—and a hundred skiers are milling around you. Stretch your legs forward, backward, and sideways. Stretch your sides, and shake out your arms. The starter's getting ready, so move closer to the starting line and jockey for position. Sidestep one way, then the other way, looking for a clear line. Countdown begins . . . five, four, three, two, one, go! Double pole at the start, step around that slow guy, double pole again, go wide to avoid the pigpile. You're in the clear! Start skating. Pole and skate, pole and skate. Corner coming up, skate around the turn. Another turn the other way, so skate it. Double pole on the straightaway. Steep downhill coming. Skate without poles over the rise and into a tuck on the descent. A sharp turn at the bottom, so skate it . . . whoa! Stood up too soon, so balance on one leg and then down into a tuck again'' (Figure 1.4).

The action continues over varied terrain for an imaginary short race—usually just a few minutes—until the skiers reach the finish line. During the exercise they travel as little as 5 feet in their designated space, but they capture the spirit of a real race. The exercise accomplishes many things quickly in an exciting fashion. The skiers warm up, practice basic skiing skills and techniques, learn which techniques

Figure 1.4. Day at the Races warm-up drill.

apply to different types of terrain, and practice quick changes in technique. This exercise, which is rich in imagery, enables skiers to visualize their moves on a race course. All skiers learn valuable skills whatever their level of development.

A major benefit of play is that participants unknowingly develop efficient technique. The activities demand that skiers perform specific tasks, and the skiers concentrate on the task rather than on themselves. In games skiers often move with partners or in a small group, and they are less self-conscious than an individual performing before an audience. As a result, participants are loose, relaxed, and willing to gamble with new ideas that promise great rewards.

Rarely does a game produce bored, fidgety children. Fun-filled exercises and activities often provide short bursts of programming that appeal to a child's sense of time. A good blend of activities captivates active children and adds interest to repetition of basic skills. Not only do children look forward to each activity by asking, "What's next?" but they also remember beneficial games to play later. Favorite games can be repeated often, offering extended practice, especially to disabled children who need greater repetition to learn a new sport.

Good games involve everyone, and the best activities are those in which every player is a winner. A noncompetitive emphasis sets the stage for new skiers to feel good about themselves. Young racers often need a break from the seriousness of competition, and games can reawaken them to the enjoyable nature of the sport. A healthy, well-rounded approach leads to the development of skiers who ski well with others and are aware of their environment.

Adults have much to learn from a child's love for games. Concentrating on completing a fun task prevents adults from getting bogged down in a preconceived image of what is correct and moves them away from the "learning-is-serious-business" approach, with which a skier develops a mental ledger sheet with credit and debit lines for mastering skiing techniques. A lighter approach moves skiers into the realm of feeling an activity before analyzing it, which gives their bodies a greater chance of memorizing the moves.

More importantly, play offers the right kind of practice. Line up young children for a windy explanation or an involved demonstration, and watch their attention and enthusiasm fade. But ask them to shadow box with a partner or experiment with one-armed wrestling on skis, and they'll ask for additional imaginative tasks. Such activities encourage skiers to use their senses of seeing, hearing, and feeling in a coordinated way that improves performance (Figure 1.5).

Figure 1.5. One-armed wrestling.

Play encourages skiers to learn by doing—and by doing a lot! This active philosophy recognizes that people learn best through a multisensory approach: the more senses involved, the more effective the learning that takes place. Play also capitalizes on the simultaneous use of the senses, which reinforces and strengthens learning.

As children experience physical sensations, they develop an awareness within their bodies of what feels efficient or inefficient. Learning through games puts children in touch with their bodies by offering lots of action, many opportunities to try again, little time to think, and few chances to make mistakes. Games create an environment for uninhibited practice.

In *The Sweet Spot in Time*, author John Jerome (1980) describes that special moment when an athlete knows that a move is perfect. The bat connects with the ball in just the right way, and the player feels the sweetness of perfection. Finding the sweet spot takes a lot of practice—perfect practice—but children have an advantage. They crave sensation, and they respond enthusiastically to tasks that require it. Children haven't cluttered their heads with too many thoughts about skiing, and they know when the skiing feels right.

These sweet, fluid motions are the mark of versatile, uninhibited skiers. Some people lose that awareness when their physical fitness suffers; they grow out of touch with their bodies. Others aren't sure if they've ever truly felt it, because they are new to recreational activities. Still others intellectualize the learning of physical skills.

Encouraging children to learn through play keeps them in touch with their bodies and heightens their sensory awareness of physical skills. An added benefit is that children are likely to play longer because games are enjoyable and challenging. They get increased practice, which lays a better foundation for their development.

This playful approach is valuable because it develops more than the physical abilities of new skiers. The activities meet the emotional needs of children and help them to grow in a healthy manner.

Goals for Play

Games on snow are energetic and often crazy. To an observer with preconceptions about organized ski programs, the action might seem too chaotic at times. What's the point in all this craziness? Shouldn't we get serious about learning to ski?

Play encourages a child to feel comfortable, to participate fully, to have fun, and to be successful in learning a new endeavor. Play doesn't happen by accident. Every successful activity has a clear purpose and a well-orchestrated plan beneath the craziness. Without these ingredients, the play is likely to be ineffective in meeting a child's needs and in developing skills.

Organizations like the New Games Foundation have increased our understanding of the value of play. The foundation is known worldwide by its motto, "Play hard, play fair, nobody hurt." Creative activities, such as those promoted by the foundation (New Games Foundation, 1981), have found enormous acceptance in the last decade as an effective alternative to traditional games and instructional methods. Many people now recognize that creative activities build better people because the focus is playing the game rather than winning it.

Gone are yesterday's disastrous ways of choosing teams with which the captains picked people until a few poor individuals were chosen last. Gone are elimination games, in which the uncoordinated kids watched from the sidelines for most of the activity. Gone are the games that spotlighted the losers.

Today we might see captains choose fair teams by new rules: people whose month of birth begins with J on one side, or everyone wearing blue on one side. Today leaders organize games that involve the entire group throughout the activity. Today a group is more likely to work together to solve a problem rather than strive for individual glory.

This renewed appreciation for playing rather than winning doesn't eliminate competition. Competition can be appropriate when it motivates players to work together and when it builds their self-confidence. It is inappropriate when it emphasizes the failures of players and when it undermines their self-esteem.

Playing on skis reminds us that skiing is fun. Children who enjoy all aspects of skiing—the mechanics of the sport, the outdoor environment, and other skiers—will love to ski. They'll clamor to continue skiing if their involvement is satisfying. Let's look more closely at how play meets the needs of children and helps to develop their love for the sport.

Physical Comfort

Play keeps children active and warm, and complaints of coldness are infrequent with well-run activities. Ski games usually create rosy faces and a pile of clothing on the sidelines on a warm day. Young children who complain they are cold and tired are generally speaking the truth. Those complaints can be a sign that activities and organization need closer examination and that the leader may need to make changes so the activities better suit the group.

Games also fulfill a child's need to move quickly in spurts. These "spurt-and-die" skiers can move all day in this manner. Feeding their craving for plenty of action requires a new approach to teaching, including lots of 30-second lesson plans! A leader's repertoire of activities needs to be large to provide many options at short notice.

Fatigue is a major factor that affects learning. A 4-year-old may ski happily for only a half hour. If forced to stay outside for a longer time, the child's lasting impression may be the fatigue of the final 15 minutes. But a short, enjoyable play period will leave that little skier wanting more (Figure 1.6).

Figure 1.6. The end of an enjoyable play period.

Confidence

Emotional well-being is difficult to assess, but its importance cannot be overlooked. Everyone wants to feel capable and confident, and children are no exception. Games diminish the intimidation that can accompany learning new skills. Total-group participation reduces observer roles and the feeling that everyone is watching an individual.

Games promote intense involvement that limits how greatly players judge their progress against others. Children have little time to keep a scorecard when they are active players rather than sideline judges. Competition is appropriate at times for motivation, but the healthiest form of competition involves individuals competing with themselves.

"Personal best" activities allow players to beat their own records and sense their improvement. Within a group, individuals can try an exercise in separate areas and measure their own progress. No one except the individual player needs to know the results: The only contest is seeing one's own improvement.

For instance, Super Pole Challenge asks the skiers to double pole between two points and count the number of poling actions. Skiers repeat the exercise and try to reduce the number of their poling actions. It's a great contest for individuals to beat their own records. Skiers will vary in their totals depending upon their type of skis, ski wax, and effective poling actions. There is no correct number, and many skiers are ready to keep trying until they can't reduce their poling actions any further.

Determining a child's emotional comfort is important. Signs of problems can be physical, like serious faces, stiffened stances, and mechanical movements. Behavioral clues might be a child's positioning in the group: always in the back (intimidated) or the last to act (nervous about performing).

Participation

Making an effort is more important than success or failure. How often do children avoid a new activity because they're afraid of holding other children back? Play focuses on the importance of participation, and it encourages the players to try to the best of their abilities. Good activities allow children of differing abilities to play together without fear that they are lagging behind. Especially effective are activities that encourage partnerships or teams of players with similar skills.

For some, the hardest step is the first one. Even children lacking in confidence are willing to participate in games after taking a few hesitant steps; they often then rush headlong into the group activities. For instance, a skiing activity in which falling down is inevitable can be an enormous relief, and skiers will relax and ski with greater comfort after that first fall.

Games allow children to develop increased comfort, coordination, and agility; they begin to feel good about their performance. Balance, rhythm, and timing are the major ingredients of smooth, flowing physical movements. People want to experience pleasure in the way their bodies move, and children are no exception.

Ski play encourages patterns of movement in which one action flows into another and the tempo of the movements may change many times. Versatility is heightened by play, because skiers move away from learning a technique for its own sake and toward an instinctive understanding of a series of movements that fit a particular situation. Children demonstrate an uncanny ability to instinctively react with a workable solution.

Sharks and Minnows is a good example of a ski game that encourages uninhibited participation. On a rectangular playing field, a shark (the instructor) begins the game by yelling "shark attack," and the minnows must ski the length of field to safety. The shark tags minnows as they ski; once tagged, minnows also become sharks. The game ends when everyone is a shark. In this game, the action on the field is intense. Sharks and minnows glide, turn quickly, and dodge other skiers while they also make important decisions about when and where to perform these moves. Developing these strategies involves an awareness of the entire environment—terrain, skiing movements that work, and other skiers.

To participate uninhibitedly, players need to understand an activity and know what's expected of them. Their understanding the rules of the game is an important prelude to becoming involved fully in an activity. These rules can move beyond specific directions about what to do; for example, some adults need to be encouraged to have fun and be reassured that playing is permissible as well as valuable. (Chaperons and parents often need to be encouraged to drop their observer's role and join the action.) Young children have few problems with that rule, but some adolescents who fear looking stupid may need encouragement. If they are unreceptive, don't force the activity or they may be turned off.

Games avoid technical jargon and confusing explanations of maneuvers. They offer a clear picture of tasks and the easy steps needed to accomplish them. Setting up this stage allows lots of performing, and the little actors get repeated opportunities to practice good skiing. This simplified mental process improves skiers' chances of success.

Interaction

Finding joy in one's own participation leads to an increased joy in the company of other people. Fun is contagious! As children feel relaxed about their skiing and themselves, they are more open to sharing the experience with others. Mutual support also develops as they become more involved in the needs of other people.

Play teaches more than skiing, and children who participate in play learn valuable social skills such as leadership, task sharing, problem solving, and coaching. Good games generate lots of chatter, laughter, cheers, applause, suggestions for variations, and requests for more!

Games require more than physical skills, and they offer children an opportunity to assume different roles. Some children are good organizers and lead their team to work cooperatively. Others are quick thinkers and can make good decisions for their group. Everyone who joins can find a meaningful role.

Cooperative activities encourage children to be sensitive to the development of others. Some adolescents discover they can be good teachers and can offer helpful suggestions to others. In skiing, this sensitivity can help to reduce the peer pressure that often accompanies dares, thus increasing the safety of other skiers (Figure 1.7).

Figure 1.7. Cooperative activities increase sensitivity to others.

Enjoyment

Pleasure is highly individual; leaders must consider each child's goals when organizing programs. While some children want to climb endless hills, others just want to be with their friends. The desire to go somewhere can be crucial to some children's pleasure. Beyond exploring new terrain, exploration can mean discovering new "hot" moves! Enjoyment often depends upon whether children's needs are being met.

Everyone likes to reflect upon an experience and see progress. But each person has a different definition of success. Bold, confident skiers, regardless of their ability, express a desire to go faster on more difficult terrain. New, timid skiers want to control their speed. Other skiers put their needs in more emotional terms—freedom from fear, confidence to try something new!

"Fun meters" are an enlightening way to ask kids to rate an activity. The ones awarded an enthusiastic 10 are often simple, silly games with an imaginative theme, which fulfill children's desire for full, uninhibited participation. These activities usually feature a challenging new move at which skiers can achieve some success. Of course, children can be ruthless in their ratings, letting the leader know in unequivocal terms when an activity is low on the fun meter. The challenge is finding the right activities appropriate for skill development, and experimentation will inevitably lead to a few duds as well as big winners.

A perennial favorite among cross-country skiers is Samurai Warrior, modeled after an original New Game, an alternative activity that develops a spirit of cooperative play (Fluegelman, 1976). A samurai (the instructor) stands in the center of a large circle of skiers who are well away from the reach of the sword (a ski pole held with grip end toward the skiers). The samurai swings the sword around the circle, alternately dipping near the ground (as skiers jump) and waving it over their heads (as skiers duck). Pointing the sword in the direction of a skier is a sign that he or she must fall down and get up quickly. Quickly changing the height of the sword's swing prompts lots of falling and laughing. Children love the game, because falling is not embarrassing and they can enjoy themselves comfortably.

A Word About Safety

Safety awareness is necessary for every skier's education, and it must be an integral part of children's programs. Skiing is a dynamic, challenging sport with inherent hazards that make it an exciting activity. Weather, terrain, snow conditions, other skiers, equipment, and a skier's own performance affect the nature of skiing.

Terrain for ski play involves factors such as steepness, snow conditions, and the abilities of the skiers. Exercises that prompt total-group action (and confusion!) are often best performed on flat terrain and gently sloping hills. One-ski exercises are miserable in fresh powder. Activities that create high-speed pigpiles are unsafe anytime.

Just imagine the intensity of a playground, with its fast action and enthusiastic players: quick turns, leaps, and jumps, building excitement, scrambling, and falling. A playground on snow has a similar intensity with an additional consideration: A skier's ability to control the speed of his or her actions is more difficult, and the action on snow speeds out of control more quickly. Safety must be the top priority in game playing and one to which all players and the leader are committed.

Young children often focus on only one aspect of a situation, and they can be unconcerned with other skiers. They may blithely cross the paths of faster skiers and enter intersections intent on their own route. They can't handle additional stimuli until they are older. The youngest skiers need a simple "one-rule-a-time" approach to increase their awareness (Figure 1.8).

The foundation for responsible skiing must be established from the beginning, and the youngest skiers cannot be exempt from their responsibilities. They need to learn how they can be safe skiers and enjoy the sport (Figure 1.9).

Figure 1.8.   While concentrating on learning to ski, a child may forget to think of others.

Figure 1.9.   Teach children safety rules early.

Resisting peer pressure is difficult for children, especially adolescents, and they need support in their decisions about their participation—particularly their choices to not participate in certain activities. Games give children alternatives to daredevil activities like high-speed chases on trails and are an important part of safety education.

Outdoor education is a cooperative venture in today's society, a venture in which leaders establish the nature of the activities and individuals determine the extent of their participation. The younger the child, the less his or her ability to make those decisions. Consequently, leaders are responsible for choosing activities suitable to the needs and abilities of their participants. As children mature, they develop greater abilities to decide the manner or extent of their participation.

This issue is an increasingly difficult one, given the rise of skiing accidents. Leaders can establish a solid foundation through programs, activities, and attitudes that encourage safe, responsible skiing. The underpinnings of this philosophy are the following basic tenets:

- Ski in control.
- Ski within your abilities.
- Know your limits.
- Avoid collisions.
- Use equipment properly.

Dick Hall, founder of the North American Telemark Organization, has a well-known playful approach to skiing, yet he is serious about safety in ski programs. He features special clinics with wonderful names like "Is There Life After Telemark?" and "Chasing Gates: The Bamboo Jungle." His "Trees Please" program takes people into radical terrain on wooded hillsides. Yet Hall combines fun with safety, and his motto reflects the New Games Foundation philosophy: "Ski hard, play fair, nobody hurt." It's a commitment that all skiers need to share.

2 The Ski Playground

A playground on snow is a delightful learning environment for young skiers. The backyard, a town park, fields, and trails at a ski area have the potential to be effective playgrounds. But the terrain alone does not create the right climate for learning to ski in a playful way; other factors are necessary to build a successful learning environment.

Important considerations are the ages of the children, the leader's style of teaching, and different types of group organization. Children change dramatically as they grow older, and these changes can affect the manner in which a parent or instructor structures the activities. A leadership style appropriate for 4-year-olds may not work with 13-year-olds. A successful circle game with preschoolers is usually too confining for energetic sixth-graders who want a larger playing field.

The nature of sports instruction has changed greatly in recent years as we have come to understand more completely how people learn. The learning by doing approach requires that we offer people many different opportunities to watch, listen, and feel. The more traditional approaches are being transformed through the addition of proven alternatives like game playing.

A revolution is occurring in skiing, so that it's often hard to identify the ski instructor amid the mass of skiers. A rare sight is the traditional line-up of students facing an instructor who commands like a drill sergeant. More common are scenes in which the instructor is a part of the group—in huddles, in follow-the-leader lines, or as a participant in the crowd.

Captain Zembo (Alderson, 1981), an alias for alpine skiing instructor John Alderson, personifies the new approach. Alderson published one of the first alternative guides to ski teaching, in which he developed the idea of a Space Ranger Demo Team. In his words, he "climbed into the skins" (p. 3) of the Rugrats (preschoolers), Space Cadets (elementary school children), and Space Rangers (teenagers) to orchestrate lots of craziness and fun at their level.

The games approach helps involve parents in the learning process in a healthy way. Many parents, regardless of their skiing abilities, have much experience in developing good games and are sensitive to the activities that generate enthusiasm with their children. That experience is invaluable in creating a lighthearted learning environment on snow.

All ski leaders, whether parents or professional instructors, need to see their instruction through the eyes of a child and organize it in that light. Age is the first important consideration in choosing appropriate activities.

Age

Children of all ages possess a natural desire to have fun, and ski play excites them about the sport as well as encourages their development. Children vary widely in their physical, mental, and emotional development, and understanding these differences is important in choosing appropriate activities for them. Their age can greatly affect their learning of a sport as well as their continued participation.

Many parents want to know the best age for a child to begin skiing and what can be expected at certain ages. Parents need to set realistic goals for their children and temper their expectations with the reality of a child's physical, mental, and emotional readiness. What a parent wants a child to learn may differ significantly from what the child wishes to experience. That difference can be crucial to the child's future participation (Figure 2.1).

Figure 2.1. Parents should set realistic goals for their children.

A ski school director experienced this problem while setting up a private lesson for a 7-year-old girl at her father's request. The girl was a beginner with relatively good balance but little experience on skis. Her father wanted a skating lesson because he had already covered the basics with her. He also talked with the director about volunteering to coach a local Bill Koch Ski Club for young Nordic skiers. The father watched the lesson and later complained that the lesson did not emphasize enough skating.

The instructor explained his strategies in meeting the child's needs: The skating had progressed nicely, but when the child became physically tired with that technique, they explored new territory for a change of pace. The girl loved skiing the hills, and the instructor finished the lesson on the hill because she wanted to practice her newly discovered turns.

In this case, the child's physical development allowed only limited practice of strenuous skating techniques. To belabor the practice would have fatigued the girl to a point where she probably would have skied poorly. The instructor capitalized upon a successful moment with the skating and then moved to an exciting, new experience for the child. Most importantly, the child was ready to return for more skiing.

Balancing the expectations of adults with the abilities and desires of children is a difficult process that should not be avoided. Instructors and program coordinators need to explain their strategies to increase parents' understanding. That this parent was unwilling to alter his original goal concerned the ski school director, and the parent's reaction raised serious questions about his role as a coach of young skiers. The director decided against the parent as a club coach, because the director doubted the man's ability to coach in a healthy, understanding manner with an awareness of children's special needs.

Understanding the abilities of pint-size skiers is a challenging puzzle with great rewards. In developing programs for very young children, Maggie Sjostrom, children's program director at Wildcat Mountain in New Hampshire, has said, "The basic goal for these lessons is to make the child want to learn to ski all by him or herself. One should not force reluctant children. . . . The main focus is that the child enjoys skiing and wants to come back to us" (Sjostrom, 1988b).

Early childhood programs emphasize a basic orientation to the sport, particularly getting used to the snow and ski equipment. An exposure to different terrain and environments beyond the backyard is also important, and visits to ski areas can be exciting steps in developing familiarity with the sport (Figure 2.2).

Separation from parents can be a problem for preschoolers, and fatigue is often a major consideration for skiers younger than 5 or 6 years of age. Parents and leaders of organized programs need to be flexible in making arrangements to meet these needs. Leaving a

Figure 2.2.   Visiting a ski area helps a child become familiar with the sport.

program early is okay! Being able to go indoors is often necessary and is more important than missing part of a program.

Team teaching is a valuable approach in skiing, because leaders can better handle differences between children. The younger the child, the fewer children should be in the program. A 1:1 ratio at the earliest ages is often necessary. Having helpful parents or volunteers to provide children with attention is often important. Helping children stand up repeatedly is time consuming, and extra hands are a welcome addition.

Each age has its special concerns. A major source of information for this section is Sjostrom's (1987) articles in *Teaching Guide for Children's Instructors*, published by Eastern Professional Ski Instructors Association.

Age 2

Two-year-olds can learn to ski under special circumstances, especially when they have opportunities to ski for short periods. Being used to cold weather is important at this age. Children who come from skiing families treat the sport as a part of family life and may already be familiar with the equipment and wintry weather.

Many 2-year-olds may not be ready for an introduction until the parents are completely tuned into their child's needs and are willing to temper their expectations. Skiing independently at this age is usually unrealistic (Figure 2.3).

Private lessons work best, in which an understanding instructor can cater to the children and ease them into a snowy land of play and songs. Standing independently and stepping are major goals. Crawling and sitting are a natural part of this experience. Children may need to simply practice walking around in the ski boots while holding poles at first. It's important to take the time to orient children to the equipment and terrain and to enable them to feel comfortable.

Hands-on attention is often necessary to reduce children's frustration. The leader can help by moving the skis or poles into place or by guiding the children's bodies through an action.

Figure 2.3. Two-year-olds need to be assisted when skiing.

Age 3

Many youngsters first express a desire to ski at this age. They are excited by skiing activities and by skiing with other children, although their skills in social interaction are just developing and need encouragement.

Some children may respond more independently to instruction than others at this age; others will need a nap. Keeping parents nearby is helpful because some children may benefit by taking a break. Communication with parents helps to set realistic expectations; participating in the program without taking a nap could be the most important consideration!

Leaders need much effort and enthusiasm to direct these activities. Organized games don't work well, but these children love mimicry and silly tasks! They enjoy following a leader into an imaginary world on snow, and then readily embrace suggestions like, "Let's bob like a jack-in-the-box." Children at this age are beginning to reach out to others, and group circles work well for directed activities (Figure 2.4).

Sjostrom notes that the average 3-year-old has short legs, a long trunk, and a large head; this child's center of gravity is high. As a result, these children tend to sit back on their skis and may have difficulty leaning their legs forward against their boots. Sjostrom recommends a maximum ratio of three children per instructor.

Figure 2.4. Imitating objects such as a jack-in-the-box is fun and educational.

Age 4

These children are becoming independent, and they want to do things for themselves. They are better able to help with putting on their own ski equipment. Their improved physical coordination makes skiing easier, but they give up easily and are sensitive to slights from their peers. Their emotions are highly changeable. The instructor needs to provide strong encouragement and to monitor the interaction of a group.

Four-year-olds are developing an awareness of their bodies and are willing to experiment. They like lots of action and fidget if they don't get it! They are more able to handle open-ended tasks or problem solving but still only in short bursts of activity. New challenges are exciting for them.

These children's imaginations are developing, and pretending to be different characters or animals is easy. Competition can be difficult, because they don't like to lose, thus activities in which everyone wins are the best approach (Figure 2.5).

Figure 2.5. Noncompetitive activities such as imitating animals work well with four-year-olds.

Age 5

This age is often the ideal time for children to learn. Their physical and emotional development is more balanced; they can handle the physical demands of games as well as the required interaction with other children. Their ability to follow directions increases along with their desire for independence. While they can pursue independent actions, a need for strong direction still remains to channel their energies.

Five-year-olds are enthusiastic about learning and are anxious to please. Their coordination allows them to move freely on skis and to make instinctive decisions about appropriate techniques for the terrain. Poles are easier to use for children at this age, and they begin to use poles for increased power. They are challenged by new tasks, and they like to experience a sense of improvement in their abilities. They are excited by their progress.

Getting along with their peers is important to them, and they enjoy activities that encourage this interaction. Partnerships and small-group activities begin to work well at this age.

Middle Childhood (6 to 12 years)

Children in these middle years have entered elementary school and have a large, new environment helping to shape their lives. The descriptions of these children are more general, because children of the same age may differ greatly in their characteristics. In *Teaching Guide for Children's Instructors* (1988a), Sjostrom notes that "all children are different and enter stages of development in the same order but not necessarily at exactly the same time."

These children are less reliant upon their parents and more oriented to their new group of peers. Interacting with friends is important, and they welcome partnerships with other children. They are willing to work independently with small groups although strong direction is still required, especially in the early grades. If they know what is expected of them, they respond well. Their independence lets them enjoy periodic unstructured "free ski" sessions, as long as safety rules are established firmly. However, they have a natural exuberance that may need to be tempered!

These children have the ability to watch each other and learn from their observations. They love follow-the-leader activities. Being able to be a leader is important in the older years, and these children willingly follow when they are assured of a turn as leader.

They also love to imitate instructors and are ready to do so quickly! These children learn through mimicry so well that they exhibit advanced technique flawlessly. It's inspirational!

Their analytical skills and their abilities to solve problems are improving. They can identify specific skills that are a part of techniques, and they can understand how a particular skill might make their skiing better.

Their energy is high, and they can ski in a "spurt-and-die" fashion for hours. By 9 or 10 years, they have the physical coordination to be strongly balanced skiers and to be challenged by advanced techniques. They know what's hot and what's not, and they are willing to try anything (Figure 2.6).

Sjostrom observes that the legs catch up with the torso proportionally, and the center of gravity begins to shift downward between 7 and 9 years of age. In the first few grades, boys are heavier and taller than the girls. But toward the later years, the girls begin their adolescent growth spurt earlier and grow larger than the boys.

Figure 2.6. Nine- and ten-year-olds will try anything.

Adolescence (13 to 16 years)

Teenagers are like preschoolers in some ways! Puberty with its corresponding growth spurts can create wide differences in physical and emotional development. The junior high school years are often a difficult period that can affect the ability to learn new skills.

Girls enter their adolescent growth spurt earlier (11 to 13 years) and usually have fewer problems with coordination as their bodies adjust to the physical changes. They can suffer a change in attitude, though, that makes sports a low priority. They begin to be more conscious of how they look and what others think of how they perform.

The growth spurt for boys is later (13 to 16 years) and causes more dramatic physical changes. Their shoulders widen, their legs grow longer in relation to their trunk and their forearms also lengthen. (Sjostrom, 1987). Boys can lose coordination at this age; they look like they're all arms and legs! They can be embarrassed by their inability to master a move as quickly as they want to (or used to be able to!).

Generally, children at this age are more self-conscious, and they may lose their willingness to experiment. Putting them on stage as individuals can be disastrous, and they prefer total-group activities in which everyone participates equally. Beware of activities perceived as too silly! Adolescents are quick to label an activity as "uncool."

Because they have an increased fear of failure, these children need to be assured of succeeding with tasks in order to enjoy the activity. Instructors must be careful with individual criticism. Lots of group praise is appropriate, as these children enjoy being a part of a good group. Give them plenty of opportunities to excel, but still challenge them with new experiences. A leader's participation with them is important, because it develops friendly interaction that is desired at this age.

Leadership Styles

How one teaches depends upon the age of the students, because children vary in their needs for different kinds of direction. A good leader is a blend of many personalities: a giant kid, a gentle taskmaster, a smooth model, a thoughtful inquisitor, an alert referee, and perhaps a touch of Attila the Hun. The greater the leader's ability to employ a variety of these approaches, the greater the likelihood of reaching more children.

A local photographer once unnerved me with revealing photographs of a fifth-grade ski lesson that I taught. In looking at these black-and-white vignettes, I saw myself in many roles—from an overgrown child participating in a game to a police officer directing the action on the hill (Figure 2.7).

Ski play involves intense action and requires different types of direction to be successful. The activities often look chaotic and appear unstructured, but the effective ones are highly structured and well planned. A leader's choice of approaches is crucial to the success of a program.

Let's look at the teaching styles outlined by Muska Mosston in *Teaching Physical Education* (1966) and examine their usefulness in various ski programs. Especially important is their relevance for children of different ages.

Figure 2.7. Acting as a police officer on the slopes is one of the many roles a ski instructor assumes.

Command

The most common style is command teaching, in which the leader is highly directive and supervises the action closely. Everyone looks to the leader for decisions, and the ability to determine the class climate rests with this leader. The participants have little or no involvement in decision making. Because the leader is the focus of this style, demonstration and explanations are commonly used to provide information.

Command teaching is valuable in ski play, in which strong direction is often needed to insure safety. As excitement and enthusiasm build, a leader needs to be able to control the action before it becomes chaos. Especially important is the decision to stop a game before safety is jeopardized. Traffic control on hills and other advanced terrain is necessary for safety, and the command mode works well in this situation, as the leader can establish a few key commands like ''time out'' and "freeze" to control the play. (Forcing players to freeze on a hill promotes great practice of their ability to stop!)

The leader should use the command style when a program has time constraints or the group is large. This style gives the leader better control over the pace of the activities and enables the leader to organize the group more effectively. The command style is generally more efficient, because more activities can be packed into the play period. Communication is generally improved, and guidelines for games can be explained clearly.

The command style is evident in large-scale games on snow like soccer, frisbee, or tag, in which the leader functions like a referee. In fact, using a whistle to stop or direct the play is invaluable.

The younger the children, the more guidance they need. However, excessive guidance can undermine their enjoyment and acquisition of new skills if it delays their desire to dive wholeheartedly into the activity. Excessive commanding can also undermine their ability to be independent decision makers.

Leaders can channel children's spontaneity and curiosity through other methods and can choose the right moments to direct the activity strongly. When the leader reserves commands for safety, children will be more likely to respond!

Leaders should use the command style in the following situations.

- With large groups
- When time is limited
- In fast-action games
- To improve safety
- With all ages

Task

A task-oriented style focuses on the participants more strongly and involves them sooner than the command style. The leader still determines the overall activity and explains or demonstrates the challenges in the specific tasks. But the children determine the nature of their involvement and can begin and end their practice on their own.

This approach fosters greater independence in decision making and involves children more intimately in the activity. The leader tells the children what to do but not how to do it. They control the intensity of their performance, how long to practice, and when to take breaks. They can repeat a challenging task or return to an earlier one if they finish before others.

The task-oriented style works well in skiing, where physical strength and endurance may differ greatly among skiers. Leaders can use tasks with groups of children of varying ages and skill levels who want a chance to perform at their own speed. This style satisfies those who need to sit back and watch a demonstration before they participate as well as those who need to jump into an activity right away to learn from the experience.

Good tasks get students involved at their own level. Here is a simple task that encourages individual performance. The leader asks skiers to descend a hill and execute a few turns, then asks them to make as many turns as possible on the hill. The leader finishes by encouraging them to make at least two turns more than their last count. This is a great challenge and a wonderful way to steer the human projectiles away from strafing runs on a hill!

Tasks work well with children who have begun to ski independently and who are ready to experiment with a good challenge. Tasks lend themselves to lots of practice, but the leader must make sure that tasks can be mastered. Tasks that are too hard will frustrate skiers, while tasks that are too easy will bore them. Short, clear tasks can be nicely challenging, and because they are easily remembered, intrigued skiers will try them again. A good sign is a skier saying to a friend, "Try this!"

However, tasks may not contribute to a skier's understanding of a skill or technique. As children grow older, they have a stronger desire to know why something works. At this point other methods that promote greater understanding are more appropriate.

Leaders should use the task style in the following situations.

- With groups of mixed abilities
- With groups of different ages
- With children who can ski independently

Reciprocal

The reciprocal style moves students beyond their role of performer and involves them in the dual roles of performer and observer. This style combines doing with seeing, and it enables partners to work together to analyze what is happening.

By watching performances, observers provide their partners with immediate feedback about the performance. The performers share what they felt. Together, the partners begin to evaluate elements of the activity.

The reciprocal style can also work on a group basis when members are willing to assume the roles of performers and observers. Performing in front of a group can be intimidating for some participants while others thrive on the exposure. The spirit of a group—whether members are generally supportive in their relationships—determines whether this style will be effective.

The reciprocal style works well in skiing as young skiers begin to develop their technical understanding of the sport. The leader may provide the initial task, but the skiers begin to function as junior instructors. Skiers should experience both roles so they know the pitfalls of performing and observing. This affords a good opportunity to develop support between children and applaud good effort. With encouragement, children can begin to develop positive coaching skills. A leader needs to oversee the observation process to make sure skiers are not overly critical.

Age is a crucial consideration here. It's a rare fifth- or sixth-grader who has the ability to be a "little teacher," and observational skills are usually not developed with any accuracy until junior high school. But these skills arrive at a delicate time! Adolescents can be ruthless critics at an age when they are very vulnerable to criticism. High school students respond well to these partnerships, especially on a single-sex basis. A leader needs to be sure that skiers are paired well by personality and that feedback is appropriate.

Matching skiers of similar abilities develops mini–support groups in which intimidation will not inhibit skiers' progress. These pairings are especially effective in satisfying greater skilled skiers who can progress at an accelerated rate. Mixing skiers of dissimilar abilities will work when the superior skier is an understanding teacher. These mixed partnerships also work well when every partnership within a larger group has a weaker and stronger skier. Then the partnerships are generally equal in their combined abilities.

This reciprocal style encourages mimicry, especially follow-the-leader schemes on trails, and can be very successful in building better skiers. Mimicry allows skiers to observe and perform without having to talk about what is happening: They analyze and evaluate the skiing mechanics with their bodies rather than their brains. This style appeals to many children who are natural mimics, especially fourth-, fifth-, and sixth-graders. As both partners ski along a trail, the following skier observes the leading skier and makes immediate changes in his or her skiing style. The following skier can also observe the leader and coach that person through the changes.

Synchronized ski dances are a good example of the reciprocal style. The leader challenges partners with the task of demonstrating five synchronized moves along a designated section of trail. The leader establishes a practice period, up to 10 minutes for capable skiers, and a time for the final performance. Wide, open trails are great for these exercises, because all teams can perform simultaneously, thus reducing any anxieties about showtime.

Leaders should use the reciprocal style in the following situations.

• For skiers with similar abilities (to reduce intimidation)
• For skiers with dissimilar abilities (to develop good coaching)
• With older children and adolescents

Guided Discovery

This process leads students through a series of steps or experiences until they reach a desired conclusion. The leader asks questions that lead to this particular end, but the participants discover the answers themselves. Their powers of evaluation are developed greatly, which increases their understanding of the activity. This style shifts the focus strongly to the student.

The guided discovery approach takes time because skiers experiment with different alternatives and accept or reject them to find the correct answer. Skiers perform the various roles of observer, performer, and evaluator throughout the discovery process. As a result, they are highly invested in the outcome.

Although the leader always lets the participants arrive at their own conclusions, the discovery approach can fail if the questions are poorly conceived. Thus the leader needs to structure the questions or clues to lead the participants to a particular end.

Skiing can be a delightful process of discovery. Even young children can experiment with various options that lead them to solid skiing. They may not be able to express why one alternative is better than another, but they know instinctively what feels right. Children like to experiment, and a leader can develop good techniques by adding one new challenge at a time. This process lends itself to consecutive practice of new skills and offers skiers a good opportunity for reinforcement of the skills introduced previously.

A short slalom course offers many opportunities to pose new questions and let the skiers figure out the answers. After each question is posed, the leader encourages skiers to perform wedge turns in light of the new information. What makes a wedge turn work (besides magic!)? Is the trick putting more weight on one ski? If so, which one? Does it help to dig in with the ski? Does skidding it across the snow help? Does steering the ski help? Can more than one skill be involved? (Yes! All four skills are involved.)

By the fifth grade, children who are given good leading questions are generally able to identify what is happening with the skis. They can draw conclusions that are based on immediate experiences. But these deductions can exceed their reasoning abilities if the questions or the tasks are too complex.

Many adolescents respond well to the discovery process and enjoy the opportunity to experiment. In fact, this approach often benefits skiers who cannot perform the maneuvers well but who have the ability to analyze the mechanics. These skiers can achieve satisfaction in fielding the questions well; their brains may provide the clue that their bodies need.

Group size can be a factor in the success of this approach. The best forum for an exchange of ideas is a small group, in which skiers can talk, listen, and ski in an organized fashion. Large groups (10 skiers or more) can be too cumbersome for this approach.

The leader should use guided discovery in the following situations.

- When time constraints are absent
- With individuals or small groups (less than 10 children)
- With older children and adolescents

Problem Solving

Problem solving is an open-ended process that encourages active experimentation by students. The leader asks a question and after providing some basic guidelines lets students solve the problem in their own fashion. Students experiment with various solutions and choose one that seems best. A problem may also have several solutions, and the virtues of each can be debated.

The students use many different roles—performer, observer, demonstrator, evaluator, and director—in the problem-solving process. A leader gains valuable insights into the personalities of the children by watching the roles they adopt. Encouraging children to gamble with new roles is an important part of their growth.

The most exciting situations are those in which children begin to pose questions to each other and share the role of director. They can also treat the leader as one of the group and assign roles to that person! Asked by a new 13-year-old "leader" to perform a particular move, I've deliberately demonstrated a glitch in my skiing style, which students have spotted! Even better, their suggested change was very appropriate.

As children play with activities that involve problem solving, their exploration leads to a wealth of ideas. They become good game leaders as they develop suggestions for variations on an activity. They're especially good at calling for changes that make an activity more challenging.

For example, slalom courses on flat or gentle terrain eliminate the variable of speed to help skiers develop better skills. But these courses can also remove some of the excitement. Children will often ask for more challenges like moving the poles closer together for tighter, quicker moves. Moving poles into an offset formation forces skiers to develop more power to glide longer.

A problem might have several solutions or none. Children with good analytical skills or who work well in groups are good problem solvers. Generally, a child's problem-solving abilities improve with age; adolescents respond well to this approach, while younger skiers would rather forget the analysis and just experience the sport.

Leaders should use problem solving in the following situations:

- With groups of all sizes
- With older children and adolescents

Group Organization

Formation of a good group is no accident. The best groups are cooperative ones, in which members enjoy each other and work well together. Unfortunately, people have learned to be unsupportive and competitive in these situations. How often have we witnessed games in which joking players berate others for missed shots and poor strategies? Many players fear that beneath the joking exterior the comments are serious.

Anxiety about performing well can affect an individual's ability to learn. Anxiety manifests itself in many ways: "That's too difficult," "I'm sure I can't do that," "They are better than I am," "I don't want to hold anyone back," or "I'll just sit this one out." Familiar sentiments, right?

Many people have lost the ability to play and enjoy an activity for the sheer joy of participation. Too many competitive elements have undermined this talent. But with encouragement to be cooperative (and few opportunities to be otherwise), people can recapture their playfulness.

Supportive leadership is a crucial model. For example, if the leader is relaxed and cheerful, the spirit is likely to be contagious. Such a leader needs to say little; subtle direction can encourage a supportive environment.

An essential ingredient is the manner in which a group is organized. Certain types of arrangements intimidate participants, while other arrangements encourage them. Let's look at different schemes for organization and examine how to implement them on a ski playground.

Individual

The most stressful performance is an individual one, in which a person performs before a group. This stage creates a situation in which the actors unconsciously wait for the applause or the boos. They can suffer acute stage fright, which causes their performance to suffer. Older children are often self-conscious about stages, and some will refuse to participate in activities that single them out (Figure 2.8).

Individual performances are especially inappropriate at the beginning of a program because they build enormous stress at this point. But they can be valuable for a person who has gained self-confidence and is ready to gamble with a solo demonstration. The right moment is usually near the program's conclusion.

Ski instruction once relied heavily on singling out skiers; for example, a skier descended a trail individually and received feedback from the instructor at the bottom. But other arrangements have proven more effective for learning. The departure from individual performances makes the leader's job harder in providing feedback, but it offers a better environment for doing so.

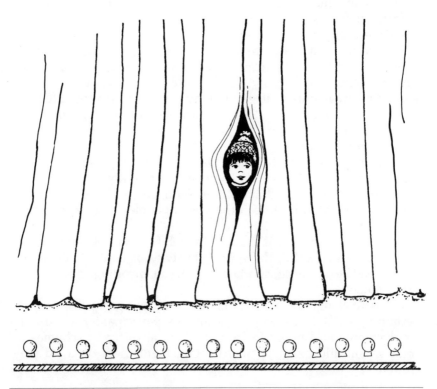

Figure 2.8.   The most stressful performance is an individual one.

Partners

Partnerships promote comfortable interaction between two students. After all, the smallest possible audience is present! This relationship can be especially important at the beginning of a program to introduce strangers. Lots of talking and laughter are good indications that children are loosening up (Figure 2.9).

Partnerships also bring people together in cooperative ways so they can share advice, commiseration, and stories about their own experiences. Children like to share their experiences with others, which adds to their enjoyment of skiing. "Hey, remember when we found that big bump and. . . ."

Partners can be paired in a variety of ways. When children choose their partners, the skilled skiers often choose each other. This pairing of equal abilities offers intense involvement and greater individual advancement, but the leader must choose activities in which these pairs aren't always the winners.

Deliberate pairing by unequal abilities offers the experienced skier an opportunity to be a good helper and the inexperienced person the

Figure 2.9. With a partner, the smallest possible audience is present.

chance to mimic a good model. These pairings can help the weaker skier to experience improved balance and more stable gliding.

Compatible personalities are important, and children who are frustrated or impatient with their partners need to be changed. (The activity also needs to be examined to see if it contributed to the frustration.)

Leaders can use methods other than measure of ability to establish partnerships; for example, by height, leg length, dominant kicking leg, hair color (let's mix!), or sex (seventh-graders will object to coed partners, but tenth-graders will approve!).

Small Groups

Separating skiers into small groups of three, four, or five can make organization an easier task, especially with energetic children. Small groups build the comfort and enhance the self-confidence of members. This organization can be used early in a program to encourage good communication (Figure 2.10).

Figure 2.10. Small groups build comfort and self-confidence.

Small groups lend themselves to many activities. The pursuit of tasks and problem solving occurs relatively efficiently. Individuals are more likely to perform well in front of a small group, and this can lead to improved self-confidence.

Leaders should use frivolous, nonskill criteria like clothing and ski color to create groups. Again, divisions by ability can be apparent to children, and such divisions are usually inappropriate in small-group activities in which the groups must interact. Establishing groups of "winners" and "losers" is disastrous in developing playfulness. Leaders should build teams, not heroes!

Separating children by similar abilities can work when the groups function independently in performing the activities. Then each group can participate at a speed appropriate for members. Adolescents who don't want the pressure of keeping up with others are particularly receptive to these divisions.

Relay races have traditionally been a small-group activity, but they can be demoralizing and counterproductive if the contest is one of speed. Plus, speed can thwart good skiing technique. Leaders should consider a different kind of relay, in which each team has a different course and their race begins at different times. In this way, no one can keep track of another team's time clock or make comparisons.

A good goal is improvement in overall time in completing the relay. Between the first run and the final one, the leader can help each skier with suggestions for improvement.

Total Group

The least stressful organization involves all members of a group participating simultaneously: No one is an audience, rather everyone is a performer. Total-group activities are extremely effective icebreakers at the beginning of a program; they help bring children together and reestablish communication after small-group activities. At the conclusion of a program, total-group activities establish a sense of unity and provide a formal statement that the program is ending (Figure 2.11).

The leader's participation helps to create a relaxed atmosphere. A successful leader is one who shouts encouragement to other players while skiing madly! A leader must be willing to act as a player as much as possible, because being only a director establishes an observer's role.

Games are great for total involvement. They keep skiers moving and warm while improving skiers' skills without their noticing it. However, games can be chaotic and tiring, and individuals may need a break from them. Rest periods and time-outs are important.

A good mix of activities is best! A leader can begin with a total-group game to get the action rolling, give everyone a task to do individually,

Figure 2.11.   Total-group activities establish a sense of unity.

divide students into small groups for a problem-solving situation, then bring everyone back for another large game.

Sensing which scheme is needed at the right moment is the mark of an excellent leader. Each group has a unique personality, and a leader must be willing to change an original game plan if a particular group is not working together well. Having a lot of tricks helps, and an openness to new ideas is essential.

Physical Arrangements

Once leaders decide the basic organization for an activity, they need to consider the physical arrangement of the group. How people are spaced in a group can affect their participation and ultimately their ability to learn. Playing on skis usually requires a departure from the more traditional line-up of skiers.

Many people, conditioned by past educational practices, assemble themselves in a straight line, face their instructor, and wait for the next directions. When encouraged to form a circle (with the instructor as part of the circle), they still leave a gap between themselves and the instructor. I try to dispel the tacit notion that the instructor is different and perhaps unapproachable by saying, "Come closer so that we can talk without shouting." I suspect that some people would feel uncomfortable if I said, "Come close enough so that I can touch you."

Children vary in their responses, which often reflect the organization of their school classroom. Some groups form the traditional single-file lines, while others choose to cluster themselves. But children are more willing than adults to blur the line between teacher and students when encouraged to do so. In fact, they'll stand on the teacher's skis in their excitement when they want to talk.

How skiers place themselves within a group can be related to how they view themselves. These physical relationships are not only an indication of a person's psychological comfort, but they can also forecast how skiers may learn. It's revealing to note which children fade to the relative anonymity of the back of the group (they need to watch first), which stand consistently near a friend or relative (they need the security), and which are first in line to try a move (they are willing to gamble and need to be active).

Underlying every choice in group arrangement is a concern for safety. The best places to ski or to stop as a group are those that minimize conflicts with other skiers. The leader should avoid

- intersections,
- crowded trails,
- run-outs at the bottom of hills,
- icy areas, and
- poorly groomed areas.

Not only are these locations unsafe, they interfere with the skiers' abilities to concentrate and to perform.

Arranging the skiers in specific ways can ease their discomfort and enhance their learning. The following material describes the usefulness of various physical arrangements on the ski playground:

Line-Up. This traditional method is still an appropriate start because it eases communication, which helps to organize the program and begin it efficiently. Because this method tends to create an invisible line between the leader and the group, the leader's communication is like a speech. The line-up is often associated with command leadership (Figure 2.12).

On the hills, the leader can use a call-down system by standing at the bottom of a section and calling for each skier to descend. The system increases safety, individual critiques, and performance anxiety. Informal arrangements create a lighter atmosphere.

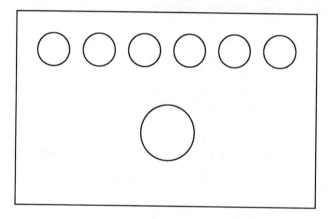

Figure 2.12.   Line-up formation.

Semicircle. The traditional line of students begins to surround the leader in a more informal fashion. The leader and students begin to relate more warmly, and communication becomes more conversational (Figure 2.13).

Leader in the Center. This more intimate arrangement brings skiers close together so they can see every face in the group. It also focuses attention on the instructor, who can provide direction easily. Experienced leaders learn to talk or demonstrate while constantly changing their position to increase eye and voice contact. The changing action is visually exciting because it provides skiers with new things to watch (Figure 2.14).

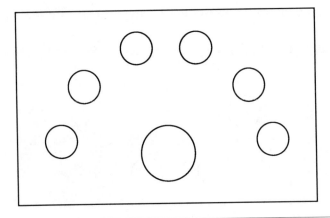

Figure 2.13. Semicircle.

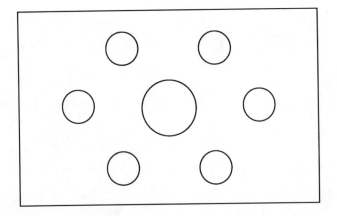

Figure 2.14. Leader in the center.

Leader on the Circle. This arrangement brings the skiers and the leader closer together and makes the leader a member of the group. The leader's participation encourages intimacy, better communication, and total participation. Skiers are motivated to join in. Activities can be initiated easily and directed conversationally when necessary (Figure 2.15).

Randomness. The leader and skiers use a free-form arrangement in their skiing activities. This highly informal approach encourages uninhibited participation and experimentation. Experienced leaders use this approach well to develop rapport and excitement in a group, but they need to be ready to adopt more formal arrangements when necessary to redirect the action.

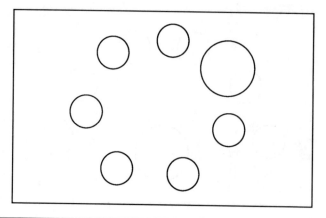

Figure 2.15. Leader on the circle.

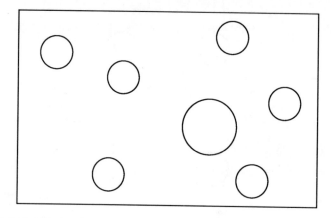

Figure 2.16. Random formation.

On hills, this free-form approach gives the leader an opportunity to watch the group in a natural atmosphere. The leader can ski down and watch from the bottom, which provides the group with a model to follow, or the leader can stay at the top, watch the class descend, then ski down. This gives the skiers a reference against which they can compare their own performances (Figure 2.16).

Experience in leading ski activities will dictate which arrangements a leader chooses in the beginning. New leaders feel comfortable with more formal group arrangements, because safety and communication are easier to develop. With some experience, however, the more informal arrangements are worth some experimentation. They lend variety to a program and offer more rewarding involvements with young skiers.

C H A P T E R 3 *Fundamental Skills*

Most children want to dive into skiing and master the different maneuvers immediately. They watch other skiers turning smoothly or remember the magazine images, and they want to do the same thing—the sooner the better, too! They want to spend little time on the basics, and that can slow their progress.

A quick way to achieve efficient skiing is to focus on skills before maneuvers. When skiers understand that skills are the building blocks of efficient moves, they are willing to devote more time to their practice. The learning of these simpler skills leads to a more successful mastery of maneuvers.

A skill is an ability to use one's hands or body with dexterity. A skill usually focuses on proficient use of one part of the body. For example, the abilities to glide on both skis or on one ski are important skills in skiing; they are the foundation for many physical actions in the sport (Figure 3.1).

By contrast, a maneuver is more complex, because it requires a unique combination of skills. For example, a sidestepping maneuver involves the skills of balancing on one leg, transferring weight from ski to ski, and often some edging and poling. The greater the number of required skills, the more complex the maneuver and the more difficult it is to learn. Turning their skis is often difficult for beginners, because the action requires a smooth incorporation of many basic skills. Once skiers look at their performance in these terms, they can understand why some moves are easier to learn than others.

Skills make learning easier, because they establish a few simple concepts that remove the mystery from the sport. Beginners begin to understand clearly which ingredients are important and how they are the foundation for all moves. Skiers begin to see that the same old skills are just refined in different ways to create new moves.

As a result, the skills approach offers skiers a greater chance to measure progress. It's a process that offers many rewards to skiers,

Figure 3.1.   Gliding on one leg is an important skiing skill.

who can take pride in performing several underlying skills even if they can't consistently demonstrate skiing maneuvers. In such cases skiers haven't failed completely; instead, they have succeeded partially! More importantly, they understand which skills need improvement to master the move, so they have a means to obtain their goals. What great motivation to continue skiing!

The skills approach has been the hallmark of American ski instruction for almost 2 decades as sports professionals have discovered more completely how people learn best. We've realized that most people cannot easily grasp complex physical moves and that they differ greatly in their manner of learning. The focus has moved from the traditional instructor in a directed classroom to a more experimental student-centered laboratory in which the leader recognizes differences between individuals.

Learning through play is a part of the evolution because it offers an excellent opportunity to focus on specific skills. Each lighthearted game or exercise is a valuable opportunity to strengthen one or more basic skills. A game's success with children lies in its appeal to a young skier's natural curiosity and need for action. Thoroughly captivated by the spirit of an activity, children may be oblivious to everything except their pure enjoyment. Meanwhile, they're developing the important skills that will make them versatile skiers in a very short time.

How does learning through play work? Let's look at one example of how a maneuver can be defined by skills and introduced through light activities. This stationary exercise encourages active experimentation, an approach to which children will respond eagerly and with astonishing results.

Many children want to descend a hill within seconds of being on snow, and they are highly motivated to learn downhill skills. When turning is introduced, they respond well to a few quick, fun suggestions that help them to discover how a ski turns. By experimenting with different ways of turning a ski, they can feel which parts of their bodies and their skis contribute to the turn.

The basic task is simple—plant a ski pole between the ski tips and press one ski against the pole. The first step is the Big Toe Theory of Turning, with which the skier presses one big toe against the inside of the boot, which is pressed against the ski pole. The toe points in the direction the skier wants to go. The task encourages the skier to rotate the foot, which in turn begins to rotate the ski. The skill learned is steering.

The next step is Knees Please, in which the skier drives the knee as well as the toe against the pole. Pressing with the knee adds a little extra oomph to the pressure against the pole and helps the skier steer more effectively (Figure 3.2).

This exercise encourages an understanding and practice of the skills that help to turn a ski—in 45 seconds! The exercise accomplishes this through a few clear directions, immediate practice, and an awareness of the body's effect on the skis. Leaders can take the exercise to a hill and coach the skiers with their turns, telling skiers to steer first with the Big Toe Theory and then take a second run using Knees Please.

This exercise is one of many that are effective for both Alpine and Nordic skiers, because the skills needed to turn are the same in each discipline. Let's look at this relationship more closely.

Alpine Versus Nordic Skills

Although the sports have their own special characters, Alpine and Nordic skiing share many similarities. As William Hall stated in *Cross-*

Figure 3.2. Big Toe Turning and Knees Please help a skier steer the ski.

Country Skiing Right (1985, p. 95), ''all skiing developed from one seed and, with time, has grown into a large tree with many branches and plenty of foliage.''

Skiing is skiing, and the basic movements remain the same. The differences are largely a matter of equipment, terrain, and vocabulary—not of form. Alpine skiing primarily involves the learning of downhill skills to control momentum on steeper terrain. Nordic skiing requires both uphill and downhill skills, because these free-heeled skiers need to create momentum as well as control it. Nordic downhill skiing is a popular hybrid that meshes all aspects of Alpine and Nordic skiing.

Each sport uses similar fundamental skills that are the building blocks of sound technique. Skiers blend these learned skills into a flow that moves their skis across the snow, and the result is the execution of similar maneuvers. Equipment dictates some subtle changes, particularly with Nordic skiers, whose heels are free to lift from the skis.

But differences in equipment cannot alter a basic fluidity of motion that characterizes skiing in general. Tony Forrest, coach of the National Nordic Demonstration Team for Professional Ski Instructors of

America, illustrated that point when Nordic downhill skiers used a mix of parallel and telemark turns on a downhill run. He used his hand to block his view of their bodies below the knees.

"You cannot tell the difference between Alpine and Nordic skiers. Their bodies above the knees are doing the same thing. They are merely finishing the turn with their feet in different positions," said Forrest at an instructional clinic at Pico Mountain in Vermont (Figure 3.3).

Figure 3.3. Can you tell the Alpine from the Nordic skier by looking at the upper body?

However, a significant difference between the two sports is the respective languages with which skiers identify the skills and describe the maneuvers. Alpine skiing is generally more technical, and numerous textbooks analyze its moves in great detail. Nordic skiing is a relative newcomer in the modern skiing world—half the age of Alpine skiing—and it's a sport in its infancy. The Nordic dictionary differs from the Alpine counterpart, although each essentially describes the same actions.

This chapter will establish a means for active practice of skiing with minimal use of technical language. The descriptions of skiing skills are intended to be brief, simple illustrations of basic concepts in skiing. The language is drawn from both the Alpine and Nordic dictionaries with no attempt to fully represent each one. Because children are often confused by technical language, it's best to use body language instead of spoken language, images instead of terms.

Using the Practice Activities

"Practice makes perfect" is better stated, "Perfect practice makes perfect." The activity and the terrain must allow the skier as much perfect practice as possible. The arena must be conducive to developing good skills, so skiers don't go too steep, too fast, or too hard too soon!

Ski play is no exception. Its lighthearted nature could lead skiers to forget that good practice of skills and maneuvers is the goal of the activities. The following hints for the leader can make skill practice successful for skiers:

- Keep fun a priority.
- Strive to keep skiers physically and mentally "loose."
- Begin on flat terrain.
- Develop initial comfort through stationary exercises.
- Develop basic ski control on flat or gentle terrain.
- Practice on hills when skiers have mastered basic ski control.
- Eliminate poles when they compromise safety.

Every skill and maneuver in this book is defined simply in descriptive terms that the leader can use with young skiers. More involved explanations are generally for the leader's or an adolescent's increased understanding. Each description is followed by basic exercises to get skiers started, activities for partners and small groups, common problems, and corrective exercises.

The exercises are listed from easiest to more difficult. I encourage leaders to begin with the easiest exercises and to modify all programs to meet the needs of their particular group. In some instances, the leader might want to change the name of an activity for an older group. For instance, a Bobbing Birds exercise for 5-year-old children might become Bow to Your Partner for junior high kids.

The nature of the students' involvement with the imagery may also change. Young children delight in quacking as they waddle uphill like a duck, and they'll immerse themselves fully in this play. Adolescents would recoil in horror at the invitation, yet they'll still understand the image of "walking like a duck."

The Basic Skills

Understanding skiing is easier when the list of skills is short and when simple words allow skiers to almost immediately grasp what they need to do. These eight skills give a skier the tools to handle two major tasks: developing and controlling speed. The basic skills are sliding, gliding on one ski, moving from ski to ski, poling, gripping or pushing off (Nordic only), skidding, edging, and steering.

Alpine and Nordic skiers vary in their use of these skills because of the differing equipment and terrain. For instance, Alpine skiers might focus on steering (rotary movements), skidding, and edging to control their momentum. But they do not need to focus on weight transfer (moving from ski to ski) as much as do Nordic skiers, who need the skill to develop momentum in their skiing. The skill of gripping or pushing off the snow is applicable only to Nordic skiers who need it to get good traction.

An integral part of every skill is balance, what one instructor calls the "state of grace." Good balance is the most basic consideration in practicing these skills, because a lack of it makes skiing difficult and frustrating.

The All-Purpose Sports Stance

Balance is a function of what I call the all-purpose sports stance. This stance applies to a tennis player waiting for a serve, an infielder waiting for a hit, a skateboarder coasting along a street, and a skier descending straight downhill. In each sport, the players have to use a neutral, balanced stance that provides them with a sense of equilibrium. Playing the sport is just a series of departures from this solid stance. It's a powerful, stable platform from which to launch the more aggressive moves.

Telemark guru Dick Hall describes this basic position as the "Slump-O-Matic." He urges skiers to stand tall with their muscles clenched and then gradually relax until their bodies are slumped slightly.

The Slump-O-Matic is characterized by flexed ankles and knees, an upright upper body with the buttocks tucked under the trunk, and hands in front of the body. This position is an integral part of Hall's "bag of bones" theory of ski physiology. By eliminating muscle tension, skiers rest comfortably on their skeletons and avoid excessive fatigue. Their bones support their bodies rather than their muscles, which are weaker than bones (Figure 3.4).

Figure 3.4. Slump-O-Matic encourages a relaxed stance.

Rhythm and timing are related to the all-purpose sports stance. Rhythm in skiing is a fluid tempo that can be regular, almost repetitive, in its beat. Any departures from the main refrain, the basic stance, occur smoothly and may have a pattern of their own. The crucial element is smoothness, and rhythmic skiers appear smooth whether they are floating gracefully or moving powerfully.

Timing in skiing involves good judgment; the right things must happen at the right times. Skiers determine when to move from the all-purpose sports stance to perform a specific maneuver and when to regain the stance's stability to prepare for the next maneuver. Skiers can experiment with the stance to see how it affects the basic skills.

Sliding

Sliding requires that skiers glide on their skis in the all-purpose sports stance. This ready-for-anything stance allows skiers to handle changes in terrain, speed, and direction (Figure 3.5).

When sliding, the skier's legs are bent or flexed from the ankles and the knees function like shock absorbers. The entire body is relatively upright with no bending from the waist, and the hands are in front of the body. Above all, the body is relaxed.

Figure 3.5. A relaxed stance increases balance when sliding.

Basic Exercises

O *Soldiers.* Skiers stand tall with locked knees (at attention). They relax their knees and let their legs slump into a flexed position (at ease).

O *Tippy Toes.* Skiers roll onto the balls of their feet until the heels of their feet lift inside their boots. They then roll onto their heels until their toes lift against their boots or binding. They settle in the middle again.

O *Reach for the Sky.* Skiers stand on tiptoes, then settle onto equally weighted feet.

O *Teeter-Totter.* Skiers rock back and forth from the balls of their feet to their heels, then settle onto equally weighted feet.

O *Hokeypokey.* Skiers jut their buttocks backward, then tuck them into place under the upper body with their shoulders, hips, and ankles "stacked" above each other. (Skiers can sing, "Jut your rear end out and you shake it all about" to the tune of "The Hokeypokey"!)

O *Touch Your Tongue.* Skiers press their shins against the tongue or front of their boots, experimenting with slight pressure and extreme pressure to obtain differences in the degree of knee and ankle bend (Figure 3.6). They can touch their real tongues at the same time!

O *Flea Leaps.* Skiers jump into the air and softly settle into a balanced position.

O *Shuffle Walk.* Skiers take several shuffling steps and settle into a balanced position while sliding on both skis. A wide stance and side-by-side position of the feet create better balance.

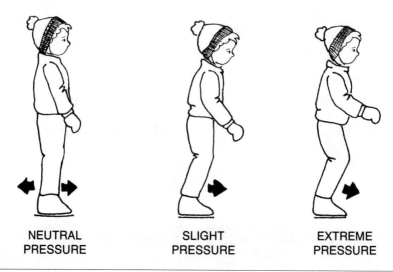

NEUTRAL PRESSURE   **SLIGHT PRESSURE**   **EXTREME PRESSURE**

Figure 3.6. Touch Your Tongue builds awareness of knee and ankle bend.

O *Partner Pushes.* A participant who isn't wearing skis pushes another skier slowly, then faster, across the snow. The skiless partner pushes against the skier's hips so the skier can maintain a good upright stance. (Pushing against the skier's back knocks him or her into a bent-forward position.)

O *Rubber Knees.* Skiers descend a gentle incline; using ''rubber'' knees and ankles helps to absorb the bumps.

O *Slide Tall, Slide Small.* Skiers descend a gentle incline, exerting slight pressure on their boot tongues by bending their legs slightly. They then descend with extreme pressure by bending their legs greatly.

Activities

△ *Pushaways.* Two partners face each other with a wide stance for solid balance. They press their hands together and try to push each other off balance (Figure 3.7).

△ *Sliding Trees.* Half of the skiers become ''trees,'' and each tree has a partner who pushes against the tree's hips. (The pushing partners take off their skis.) The trees can be moved into various formations on flat terrain, such as groves, straight lines, or clear cuts, or they can flank a long road. They can also be different trees: stately elms, swaying willows, or bushy pines. The leader can call ''Timber!'' when it's safe for the trees to topple over. Skiers who are timid about hills enjoy this activity, as it provides the sensation of sliding on the safety of flat terrain.

Figure 3.7. Pushaways test the stability of a stance.

△ *Change of the Seasons.* Skiers slide downhill by crouching (spring), standing tall (summer), then crouching and falling (fall). Young children love to pick a favorite flower and mimic its growth through the seasons. This is a nice introduction to controlled falling.

△ *Jack-in-the-Box.* Skiers slide downhill and pop up and down.

△ *Alternate Jack-in-the Box.* Two skiers slide downhill holding hands. One person pops up, while the other crouches down. Skiers try to change positions smoothly.

Common Problems and Corrections

Problem	Description	Correction
Pogo Sticks	Skiers have stiff, straight legs.	Skiers flex their knees and ankles to create shock absorbers (Slinkies).
Hinging (like the lid on a box!)	Skiers are bent at the waist.	Skiers stand tall like soldiers and stack their heads, waists, and feet like skyscrapers.
Waving Hands	Skiers' hands are too high or erratic.	Skiers rest their hands comfortably on their thighs or low on their hips (Six-Shooter Stance) to improve balance.
Leaning Tower	Skiers lean backward.	Skiers find a balanced, flexed position by teetering back and forth, then settling into a stable flat-footed position.

See the section on straight runs in chapter 5 for additional exercises.

Gliding on One Ski

Balancing on one ski is essential to skiing and requires a greater commitment than sliding. The body is centered over one ski with its weight evenly distributed between the ball and heel of the foot. Skiers must shift their weight completely over one ski so that the other ski is entirely unweighted (Figure 3.8).

Gliding on one ski is very important to Nordic skiers, who need to balance on each leg as they stride forward. It can be a difficult skill for children with poor balance. Alpine skiers tend to focus on independent leg action later in their learning of more advanced maneuvers.

One-ski exercises are important for skiers with limited balance, and the following ''scooters'' are fun! Taking off one ski enables a skier

Figure 3.8. Gliding on one ski.

to concentrate on one leg at a time. The security of a helping foot speeds up the development of good balance.

Starting with one-legged games is great because it increases a skier's control, and children can avoid the stumbling and falling that often accompanies a first time on skis. If the skier does fall, he or she needs to untangle only one ski to stand up!

Basic Exercises

O *The Stork Stance.* Skiers stand on one of their legs and stay balanced. Skiers can extend their hands sideways to maintain balance but should strive to move their hands in front of their bodies. Skiers can try this exercise with closed eyes or try to determine if one leg is stronger than the other.

O *Rubber Leg.* Skiers stand tall on one ski, then relax the leg they're standing on and let it slump into a flexed position at the knee and ankle.

O *Touching the Tongue.* Skiers stand on one ski and press their shins against the tongue or front of their boots. Skiers can experiment with slight pressure and extreme pressure to feel differences in the degree of knee and ankle bend.

O *One-Legged Pops.* Skiers pop or spring off one bent leg and land on it again. Skiers can use increasingly bigger pops to test their balance.

O *Bobbing Stork.*   Skiers stand on one ski, bend forward, and stand upright again with their shoulders, hips, and ankles stacked above each other. Skiers bob like birds on one leg!

O *Flying Stork.*   Skiers jump into the air by pushing off with both legs and landing on one leg.

O *Back Leg Lifts.*   Skiers extend one leg rearward and off the snow, then without putting weight on that leg slide it into position next to the other leg. Skiers repeat exercise using other leg. The upper body tilts forward during the lift as a counterbalance but must return to a relaxed, relatively upright position as the leg slides into position. This is a good stretching exercise! Two partners can mimic each other as if they are looking into a mirror (Figure 3.9).

Figure 3.9. Back Leg Lifts stretch leg, arm, and chest muscles.

O *Front Leg Lifts.*   Skiers modify the back leg lift by extending each of their legs forward. Skiers can try extending each leg sideways but should always return to a relaxed, upright stance.

O *Pendulum Swings.*   Skiers swing one leg from front to back, swinging the leg vigorously and feeling the imbalance in the extreme positions.

O *Ski Scooters.*   Skiers remove one ski and use that free foot to push the other ski along. They switch gliding legs to work both legs.

O   Repeat the exercises on a gentle slope. If the speed is too dis-concerting for skiers, the leader must find gentler terrain or a shorter stretch. Return to the flats until everyone's balance improves.

O   *Toe Lifts.*   Skiers glide on one ski on a gentle slope, lifting the toes of the other foot. The ski tip lifts slightly while the tail steers like a rudder. This exercise increases control for skiers who have difficulty sliding downhill entirely on one ski. This is a nice intermediate step (Figure 3.10).

Figure 3.10.   Toe Lifts improve one-ski balance.

Activities

△   *Flea Leaps.*   Skiers stand on one of their legs and leap into the air. The leader marks the highest leap by holding up a ski pole and encouraging skiers to pop higher. Skiers should try to leap as quietly as a flea to encourage control and to discourage flailing!

△   *Russian Folk Dancing.*   Skiers stand on one of their legs and sink low, low, and lower by flexing that leg. They switch to the other leg while crouched and push high, high, and higher by extending the leg. Skiers can create a Russian dance. They should maintain good spacing in a group, because this exercise involves lots of falling!

△ *Freeze Ballet.* Skiers strike different ballet poses while balanced on one leg. Skiers wear both skis and can touch down periodically for stability. Skiers strive for flowing moves between poses. The leader calls "freeze" to see how long the skiers can stay balanced in their poses.

△ *Freeze Dancing.* This is a variation on freeze ballet for the kids in the crowd who like break dancing. The performances can be wonderfully talented!

△ *One-Ski Scooter Races.* This is fun with partners! One skier holds onto a friend, and they race between points. They can try an obstacle course around trees, traffic cones, and ski poles.

△ *Good Glide Races.* These are fun, one-ski races with a partner. The winning pair takes the fewest steps between points by gliding the longest with each push. The leader can hold a rematch and encourage each team to go for their personal best.

△ *One-Ski Long Glide.* Skiers line up side by side on a starting line, ready to descend a gentle incline on one ski. They push off hard and glide as far as possible on one leg. Each skier marks the spot (with a hat or mitten) where the other foot touches. Skiers repeat to find out who can improve their glide and go the farthest. Every skier should have his or her own "lane" to avoid collisions.

Common Problems and Corrections

Problem	Description	Correction
See Common Problems and Corrections for sliding and repeat exercises here for each leg.		
Weak Ankles	Skiers roll their skis onto the inside or outside edge.	Skiers return to gentler terrain where they can relax. Leader checks to make sure the skiers' upper bodies are "quiet" in their actions.
Dominant Legs	Skiers favor a stronger leg (often the leg that kicks a ball).	Skiers exercise each leg and work the weaker leg harder or longer to build comfort and strength.

Moving from Ski to Ski

Moving from ski to ski involves a transfer of weight from one ski to the other one. Good weight transfer often involves quick, crisp, controlled transitions between skis. The skier stands on only one ski at a time for a complete weight transfer.

New skiers want both skis on the snow at all times—the more firmly the better! Beginners with poor balance often compromise their weight transfer by straddling their skis and shuffling along in the snow.

Leaders can encourage crisp weight transfer by having skiers balance on one ski (using poles for balance if needed) and lift it immediately as the other ski touches the snow. Skiers can be "quiet" and "loud" in dampening and exaggerating the effect (Figure 3.11)!

Figure 3.11. Moving from ski to ski.

Basic Exercises

O *Sizzling Snow.* Skiers, while remaining in one place, spring from ski to ski, keeping only one ski on the "burning" snow at a time. Young children like to hiss like a sizzling fire.

O *The Runner.* Skiers run in place on the skis, changing the tempo from slow to fast. Next they try running "softly" to avoid bobbing or bouncing.

O *Poison Peanut Butter.* Skiers take a step to the side, then take one the other way, keeping only one ski on the snow at a time. Quick! Don't let the peanut butter stick!

○ *Giant Steps, Baby Steps.*   Skiers step to the side, then change directions, with only one of their skis on the snow at one time. They take bigger steps, then smaller steps. The leader asks which feels better. (The smaller ones do—more control!) Skiers step faster and faster.

○ *Taller, Smaller.*   While walking, skiers bend or extend their legs to become taller or smaller.

Activities

△ *Rocking Ice Cube.*   The body is a square ice cube, and the skis form the bottom edges. Skiers tip from edge to edge (ski to ski), then slide each ski forward slightly and rock onto each ski. This exercise can create stiff skiers. The leader can ask them to "melt around the edges" to smooth out the weight transfer.

△ *Walk Like a Duck, C3PO, the Tin Man.*   Skiers walk as directed, then try it on a gentle downhill slope. The leader asks them to walk like a favorite animal, cartoon character, or story animal.

△ *Roadrunner.*   Skiers run like the Roadrunner, then try the exercise on a slight uphill slope.

△ *Step-Overs (flats).*   Skiers walk or ski forward, then step over an obstacle like a bamboo pole, flagging, a ridge of snow (Snow Snake), or ski tracks (Railroad Tracks). The leader can create a long course that makes skiers move in different directions (Figure 3.12).

Figure 3.12. Step-Overs develop quick weight transfer.

△ *Step-Overs (hills).*   Skiers slide downhill and step over a mitten, a ridge, or ski tracks. The leader should make the obstacle soft and low to the ground. Skiers often fall when they try to step over.

Common Problems and Corrections

Problem	Description	Correction
Shuffling	Skiers have poor one-legged balance and cannot shift their weight completely onto one ski.	Skiers practice lots of one-ski drills.
Short Glide, Quick Tempo	Again, skiers have limited comfort on one ski.	Skiers return to the one-ski exercises. A quick tempo will tire a skier.

Poling

Poling is a planting of the poles that increases a skier's momentum or that guides a skier through a turn. But differences exist in the way that Nordic and Alpine skiers use their poles.

Nordic skiers use longer poles for a longer push that gives them more continual power. Good poling for Nordic skiers uses the body, not just the arms. The small muscles of the arms tire more easily, and using the abdominal muscles of the torso gives greater power.

Children who are skiing independently love double poling (simultaneous action) and use it naturally. Alternate poling (like the arm swing when walking) is harder for them, and they use the poles like crutches at the beginning. Poles that are too short are often a problem; the pole needs to be long enough to be angled in the direction the skier is moving (Figure 3.13). The arms swing like a pendulum arc— down and past the knee.

Alpine skiers use shorter poles and more upright pole plants around which they pivot. These pole plants signal the ending of one turn and the beginning of another. The plants establish a comfortable rhythm that leads to good turning; they also help to face the torso downhill in anticipation of the next turn (Figure 3.14).

Children find it easy to ski without poles and love the freedom that this allows. Young children can climb uphill quickly when unhindered by poles. Leaders should introduce poles when a child has mastered basic skills without using the poles as crutches. Poles are a safety problem for unsteady beginners as well as in high-action activities and games where poles should not be used.

Leaders shouldn't analyze poling; skiers can stiffen up. Poling will happen naturally when skiers are skiing rhythmically.

Figure 3.13. Poles need to be long enough to angle in the direction the skier is moving.

Figure 3.14. Alpine skiers use pole plants.

Basic Exercises

O *Clock Pendulums (alternate poling).* Skiers swing their arms back and forth like alternate pendulums on a clock. Then they extend their arms forward as high as shoulder level, brush arms past the knees, then extend arms backward as far and as high as possible. The clock can tick slowly and quickly, wind down, and stop.

O *Pumping (alternate poling).* Skiers pump hard with their arms, letting their whole bodies move loosely with their arms. The poles shouldn't fly around but should stay in line with the skis.

O *Bowing (double poling).* Skiers extend their arms forward until they are straight and relaxed, then swing them in an arc and extend them backward and as high as possible. Skiers bend over from the waist and let the upper body follow the arms for more power.

O *Wrist Flicks (downhill poling).* Skiers flick their wrists forward to swing the poles into position. (The forearms should move a bit, but not much!) Skiers should develop a good rhythm in alternating the flicks (Figure 3.15).

O *Flick-Ups.* Skiers flick one wrist and let the body rise, then sink down and flick-up on the other side. Skiers touch the snow on the next practice and pole rhythmically. (Some kids call this one "trash collecting"!)

Figure 3.15. Wrist Flicks encourage efficient pole plants.

O   *Pole Walks.*   Skiers walk and pole without wearing skis (flats) and then run with the poles. This develops good rhythmic alternate poling for both Nordic and Alpine skiers. Skiers turn corners or try an obstacle course.

O   *Walking 'Round the Pole.*   Skiers walk along (without skis), plant one of their poles, swing around that pole, and then plant the other pole on the other side. Skiers should try for nice, effortless alternate pole plants. They can try this exercise on a hill.

O   *Touch-Turn.*   Buzzwords help to develop a good rhythm with poling. Skiers can say "touch" when they plant their poles and "turn" as they pivot their skis. "Up" and "around" are good keys, as are "bang, bang" for pole jabs, or "pat, pat" for soft touches.

Activities

△   *Power Poling (flatland).*   Skiers push with their poles to slide on their skies, keeping their feet in a side-by-side position. Skiers can experiment with double poling and alternate poling. This is not an activity for new or deep snow!

△   *Gear Shifts (alternate or double poling).*   Skiers bend their arms in "first gear" to get started. (Bent arms give greater power.) They extend their arms slightly in "second gear" when moving and extend them fully in "third gear" when flying! Skiers should let their bodies project farther forward (like a superhero) during more aggressive poling (Figure 3.16).

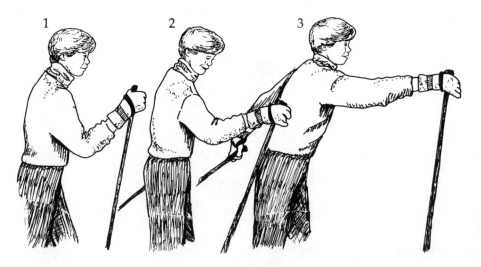

Figure 3.16.   Gear Shifts demonstrate differences in poling power.

△ *Wrist Flicks 2.*   Skiers traverse or ski straight downhill and use wrist flicks to move the poles into place. Skiers don't touch the snow. They pop forward gently on the next run and coordinate the bobbing with the poling (flick and up, flick and up). Once they establish a rhythm, skiers touch the snow on the next run. They add turns of their own choice and continue to coordinate the poling with the up-and-down movements.

△ *Reach-Outs.*   Skiers traverse a hill and reach down the hill with their poles as if reaching out to help someone. Their bodies extend downhill at a diagonal angle. This activity may involuntarily begin some good turns with children who let their skis swing around.

Common Problems and Corrections

Problem	Description	Correction
Lack of Extension (Nordic)	Poling stops at the body with no follow-through behind the body. This short, choppy poling creates a quicker, choppy ski tempo.	In double poling, skiers extend their arms backward until their hands can touch. In alternate poling, they "brush" one leg as the corresponding hand sweeps past and then lift the hand toward the sky.
Flailing Poles	Skiers have an overactive upper body and poor balance.	Skiers repeat basic gliding exercises that develop a centered body, keeping their hands low and in front of their bodies.
Excessive Arm Swings	Skiers' arms cross over their chests or behind their bodies. Excessive arm swinging forces the upper body to pivot too much and prevents quick, balanced turns.	Skiers practice Wrist Flicks to keep hands in front of the body and get the poles in place.

Problem	Description	Correction
Poor Timing	Skiers lose a sense of when poling works best if their bodies are stiff or unmoving.	Skiers loosen up their legs by rising and sinking and exaggerate the action to develop a noticeable rhythm. Then they synchronize the poling to the rising.
Stiff, Straight Arms	Stiff arms can create choppy, jabbing poling. (It can be a sign of tension elsewhere, so leaders should look for this sign in other skills, too.)	Skiers repeat the exercises with gentle poling touches, letting their grip on the poles loosen and relax. Skiers can try poling while holding the pole with only the thumb and forefinger—now that's loose!

Gripping or Pushing Off

Gripping or *pushing off* is a skill that propels a Nordic skier forward. We push off each time we walk. Good grip in skiing is aided through effective waxing of the ski or by the patterned bottom of a waxless ski biting into the snow.

The ski gripping the snow creates traction and a stable platform from which a skier can push off. As a skier pushes off, the heel lifts from the ski and the person's weight rolls over the ball of the foot; this is called a toe-off (Figure 3.17).

Figure 3.17. Gripping the snow to create traction before toeing-off.

Pushing off has traditionally been called the *kick* in a diagonal stride, but Nordic skiers are moving away from the term because its descriptive nature is limited. Using the term pushing off helps to create a powerful image of skiers propelling themselves forward and increasing their power.

Basic Exercises

O *Pops.* Skiers stand on one ski at a time and step forward, popping off each foot. They dampen the "bobbing" and pop smoothly, then spring forward.

O *Ski Jumper.* Skiers lean like ski jumpers (from the ankles) from a stationary position. One foot automatically steps forward as the other pushes off. Children like to test how far they are willing to lean before they step (Figure 3.18).

Figure 3.18. Ski Jumper develops good forward body projection.

O *Superheroes.* Children love to lean forward like Superman or Superwoman. They can test how far they're willing to lean from the ankles before they move the other foot!

O *Shuffles.* Skiers take baby steps forward and feel the balls of their feet pushing off.

O *Giants.* Skiers take a giant step forward, noticing that the pushing foot loses its strength or grip when the feet are split far apart rather than in a side-by-side position.

O *Power Pushes.* Skiers find the best spot for pushing off and taking a small, medium, or large step forward. It will be a large step if the feet are in a side-by-side position for a good push. The skier's upper body is over the leading foot.

O   *Toe-Offs.*   Skiers push off an edged ski, letting their body weight roll over the ball in a diagonally forward direction until their toes are pointed. As their heels lift, the skiers are propelled forward in a diagonal direction, like skating (Figure 3.19).

O   *The Jogger.*   Skiers jog or run on the skis like their favorite track star.

Figure 3.19.   Toe-Offs focus on strong pushing off.

Activities

△ *Cats and Cougars.*   Skiers spring forward softly like cats, then spring forward more aggressively like pouncing cougars.

△ *One-Legged Scooters.*   Skiers take off one ski and glide on the other one, pushing off with the free foot. Skiers experiment with pushing off when the feet are in a side-by-side position and with big and little pushes, noticing what happens to balance, gliding, and tempo. Balance for beginners can be better with little pushes, but their tempo increases. Glide increases with bigger pushes and tempo decreases. Skiers experiment with the differences. Which method feels better to them depends on how long they can balance and glide on one ski.

△ *Tandem Scooters.*   Each skier takes off a ski. Partners hold onto shoulders or waists for balance and coordinate their pushing feet. They put their pushing feet on the inside of the gliding skis, then the outside, striving for strong, coordinated push-offs.

△ *Tandem Scooter Races.*   Partners count the number of push-offs from Point A to Point B. They repeat the exercise, pushing off fewer times (for longer glide) or more times (for faster tempo) (Figure 3.20).

Figure 3.20. Tandem Scooter Race.

△ *Team Scooters.* In small groups of four or five, skiers practice a team scooter with everyone pushing off at the same time. They see how far each team can ski until they lose the rhythm. They ski side by side or play follow the leader.

Edging

Edging is the way the side of a ski digs or bites into the snow. The greater the tilt of the ski, the deeper it digs into the snow and the greater the edging.

Alpine skiers can edge their skis more easily than free-heeled Nordic skiers, who need to keep their feet flat on the skis and their ankles straight (instead of rolling them inward). Edging is generally a skill that a skier develops later, particularly with more advanced turns. Being able to change the edging from one side to the other side of each ski is a sign of good control (Figure 3.21).

How skiers use the rest of their bodies to edge their skis is important. Skiers who stiffen their bodies like erect trees are forced to lean their entire bodies to edge the skis. This *banking* effect requires good momentum to support the skiers, because the skis can skid out from under them when the momentum dies. Older children like to experiment with this sensation by skiing across a hill, banking sharply into it, sending up a spray of snow from beneath the skis, and risking a fall (Figure 3.22).

Skiers who treat their upper and lower bodies as independent units can control their edging better. When flexed knees and ankles are tilted sideways (as one unit), this action rolls the skis onto their edges. Meanwhile, the upper body stays relatively erect and facing forward with the skier's weight over the edged skis. The body is now zigzagged or *angulated* along its length, and the skier's weight can still apply

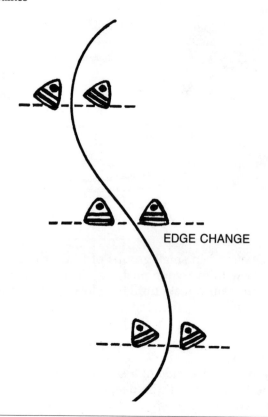

EDGE CHANGE

Figure 3.21.   Changing the edging.

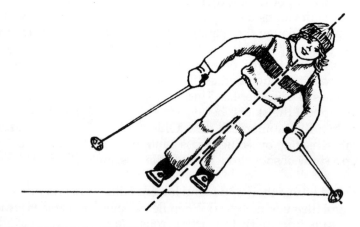

Figure 3.22.   While banking, skiers rely upon momentum for control.

pressure to the edged skis (Figure 3.23). When well-balanced skiers are encouraged to create zigzags with their bodies, they can edge their skis beautifully. A *superzag* is a sharp swinging of the knees into a steep hill!

Figure 3.23. A zigzag body shape aids controlled edging.

Basic Exercises

O *Nibbles and Bites.*   Skiers keep their skis parallel and their feet in line with their hips and shoulders for a solid stance. They can practice different degrees of edging by rolling the skis slightly to "nibble" at the snow and greatly to "bite" with big jaws. As skiers alternate edges, the leader calls out types of changes: minnows (nibbles), sharks (bites), and whales (big bites). Older children can observe the degree to which they swing their legs to edge harder, concentrating on a corresponding feeling in the feet, in which one side of the foot digs in and then the other side does.

○   *Zigzags.*   Skiers practice edging by swinging their knees from side to side. They keep their torsos upright and facing forward, striving for rhythmic swinging.

○   *Giant Steps.*   Skiers take a giant step sideways and shift their bodies above each ski. They roll from edge to edge for a nice stretch (Figure 3.24).

Figure 3.24.   Giant Steps provide a good leg stretch.

○   *Wedge Edges.*   Skiers use the A-shaped snowplow position, bringing their knees together to exaggerate the edging, then spreading them apart to moderate the effect. (Skiers can sing, ''Do your knees hang low [together], do they wobble to and fro [swing them together and apart], can you tie them in a knot [together], can you tie them in a bow [apart]?'') This moves skiers from flat to edged skis, but they must know that a knock-kneed stance signals too much edging.

○   *Rocking V's.*   Skiers use a V-shaped skating stance and roll from edge to edge.

○   *Duck Waddles.*   Skiers waddle quickly like ducks, with skis in a V shape.

○   *Bite and Release.*   Skiers stand sideways on a hill with knees and ankles rolled into the incline. They swing their knees away from the hill and slip downhill. They stop sliding by rolling their knees into the hill again.

○   *Traverses.*   Skiers glide across a hill and angle their legs into the hill for good edging. They reverse directions. Then they release the edges, slide downhill, and bite the snow again to stop the slipping.

O *One-Ski Traverse*. Skiers repeat the Traverse by gliding on the downhill ski, using the uphill ski if necessary to regain balance.

Activities

△ *Side Pulls*. Two skiers stand side by side, their skis parallel, and hold inside hands. (Their shoulders face each other.) One skier pulls the other one, who must resist by edging. They take turns.

△ *Tandem Tug-of-War*. Two skiers face their skis in opposite directions and stand side by side. (Skis can be parallel or in a wedge.) The skiers hold hands and try to force each other off balance by moving their hands. Dips, dodges, and fakes are legal! This is a great balance exercise as well. Skiers can face the other way and repeat.

△ *The Longest Leap (variation on the broad jump)*. Skiers line up their skis parallel with a starting line and leap sideways (one ski leads) as far as possible. This promotes aggressive edging!

△ *One-Ski Slalom Courses (flats)*. Skiers set up the poles in an offset fashion so the skiers must edge strongly to turn around the poles.

Common Problems and Corrections

Problem	Description	Correction
Banking	Skiers have stiff, straight legs and lean their entire bodies to edge their skies.	Skiers practice zig-zag drills and traverse hills. Gentler terrain may also relax the skiers. Vertical motion (legs like springs) loosens their legs.
Overedging	This extreme position tilts the skis too sharply and can roll the Nordic boot so that it drags on the snow. The skiers look knock-kneed in a wedge.	Skiers use sideslipping exercises on a hill with big and little "bites." They feel both extremes and return to moderate edging.

Skidding

Skidding occurs when the skis brush against the snow in a lateral (sideways) and forward motion. Skidding is a departure from the straight sliding of the skis and is a new sensation for young skiers (Figure 3.25).

Figure 3.25. Skidding is an enjoyable sensation for children.

Some degree of skidding is present in all turns. The equipment of Alpine skiers allows them better skidding control. Some Nordic skiers may have difficulty with this skill, and they appear to have no strength to sweep the skis across the snow. They often need to steer their skis well to control skidding.

Remembering to keep a flexible stance above the skis is helpful. Skiers can sink their bodies ("grow shorter") and push their skis across the snow. This sinking action drives the skis across the snow by exerting downward and sideways pressure. They can also rise ("grow taller") and lift the pressure off their skis to let them float across the snow.

After having difficulty skidding his skis, a fifth-grade cross-country skier once told me, "It's better in the air. I don't get into trouble!"

Basic Exercises

O *Ridges and Valleys.* Skiers push one of their skis sideways and leave a ridge at the farthest point, then repeat with the other ski. If one ridge is bigger than the other, skiers try to push more strongly with their weaker legs.

O *Steeps and Deeps.* Skiers press one of their skis sideways gently, then vigorously. They compare the ridges and the amount of push that is needed to create steep ridges at the end and deep valleys where the ski scrapes against the snow.

O *Angled Ridges.* Skiers push one of their skis sideways and around, simultaneously rotating the tip inward. They watch the developing ridge of snow to see if its height is uniform. Skiers push against the tip or tail of their skis to even up the ridge, then try the other side.

O *Minisprings.*   Skiers rotate both skis around, keeping them parallel and striving for a slight raising of the body to help skid the skis. They keep the skis lightly against the snow. They then change direction (Figure 3.26).

Figure 3.26.   Minisprings raise the body to help skid the skis.

Activities

△ *Stomp Fests.*   Skiers skid one of their skis furiously and repeatedly to create big ridges of snow. The leader calls out ''change'' and the skiers switch legs. The skier who creates the biggest pile wins (heavier children love this)!

△ *Hop the Line.*   Skiers hop over an obstacle (hat, mitten, pine cone, or stick) from side to side. They hop farther and farther from the item, keeping their heads and upper bodies centered over the item as much as possible and their legs under their bodies. The leader removes the item and the skiers brush the snow with their skis while hopping from side to side.

△ *Sideslip for Distance.*   Skiers sideslip downhill by braking (edging) and releasing the brakes (skidding). They try to sideslip 6 inches, then 1 foot, then more. They try for a record.

△ *Sideslip Corridor.*   The leader establishes a travel lane several feet wider than the longest pair of skis, and skiers sideslip downhill without sliding outside the corridor (Figure 3.27).

Figure 3.27. Sideslip Corridor requires controlled skidding.

△ *Red Light, Green Light.* Skiers sideslip downhill on the command "green" and stop on the command "red." Staying still on "red" encourages a quiet body. If skiers have difficulty stopping, the person giving commands can face away from the hill and turn around after saying "red." The extra time gives skiers a chance to quiet their bodies.

△ *X Marks the Spot.* Skiers spring up and swivel their skis side to side to mark an X in place. They let their skis leave the snow. Then skiers can float the skis lightly across the snow.

Common Problems and Corrections

Problem	Description	Correction
Overedging	Skiers have too sharp an edge, which digs the skis into place.	Skiers practice releasing the edges in place and brushing the skis against the snow. They try sideslipping on hills.

Problem	Description	Correction
Erratic Skidding	The skiers are not centered over their feet, so the tips or tails are pressing harder against the snow than necessary.	Skiers skid the skis flat-footed, making the snow ridges uniform in height.
Pogo Sticks	Skiers have stiff, straight legs, which have little spring to lift their skis across the snow or push them against the snow.	Skiers return to relaxed Tall, Small sliding exercises to help loosen their legs.
Overskidding	Skiers use too much steering.	Skiers return to sideslipping exercises and stay perpendicular to the hill.

Steering

Steering is the rotary force of the leg and foot that helps to turn a ski. All turns require steering, but steering is a skill that can be elusive to skiers.

Skiers should point their big toes in the direction that they want to go! To define steering this simply is contrary to other accepted and more involved definitions. But isolating rotary action this way has helped skiers understand clearly how to properly use their bodies to turn a ski.

Think of the legs as having a central axis—the big bones. Pivoting these bones also turns the foot, and the foot turns the ski attached to it. The greater the rotary motion of the entire leg, the stronger the steering.

This approach helps skiers perform subtle, strong turns like magic! A group of sixth-graders I once taught demonstrated well-steered turns by playing Star Wars and treating the skill as a special force. "Let the force be with you" was their theme.

Imagine the effect of a rousing round of "the thigh bone's connected to the knee bone, the knee bone's connected to the shin bone. . . ." The children can point to each part of their bodies as they sing the song. They should push one of their skis against the snow and feel how each part of the body works. By the time the children sing "the toe bone's connected to the ski boot" and "the ski boot's connected to the ski," everyone has experienced strong steering (Figure 3.28).

After singing this song with a group of third-graders, a mother once said, "I finally understand how a ski turns! Now I know what to do."

Figure 3.28. "The knee bone's connected to the toe bone."

Basic Exercises

O *Boot Turns.* Skiers take off their skis and turn their boots from side to side on the snow. They turn the boots gently, then sharply. They lean on their heels and point their toes from side to side. Then they lean onto their toes and swivel their heels from side to side (Figure 3.29).

O *Bag of Bones.* Skiers lift one leg and point their toes to the inside and then the outside. They watch how far the ski can move back and forth. Then they bend one of their knees and let it follow the pointing of the toes. Skiers can see how much farther their ski tips travel.

O *Big Toe Turns.* Skiers place a ski pole between their ski tips. They push one of their skis against the pole and apply solid pressure with their big toes. This toe presses against the ski boot (Big Toe Theory of Turning), and they then add their knee (Knees Please) and follow through with the hip (Hip Tricks). Children can feel the pressure build against the pole when they add body parts.

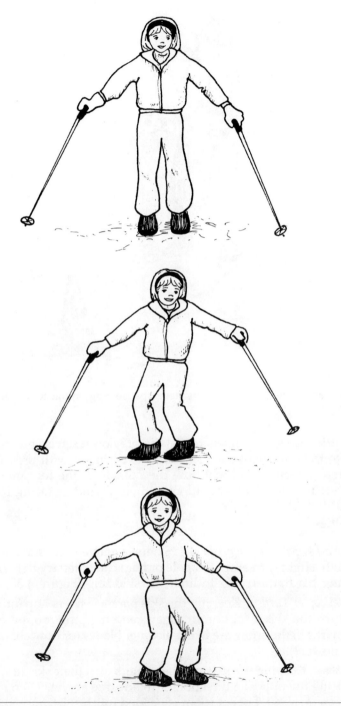

Figure 3.29. Boot Turns introduce the skill of steering.

Figure 3.30. One-Legged Steering develops steering on flat terrain first.

O *Little Toe Turns.* Skiers repeat the previous exercise but move the pole to the outside of each ski. They experiment with pressing in a different direction and feel how the outside of the foot must work to direct the ski. They should keep their shoulders facing forward.

Activities

△ *One-Legged Steering (flats).* Skiers remove one ski and scoot through a tight turn around a pole or hat. They then try tighter turns, steering hard and trying to limit the skidding (Figure 3.30).

△ *Helicopter Turns.* Keeping the skis parallel, skiers hop into the air and turn the skis a foot or so. They keep hopping around a circle. The marks in the snow are like helicopter blades (or how about petals on a flower?).

△ *180s.* Keeping the skis parallel, skiers turn their skis until skiers are facing the opposite direction (a 180-degree angle). Then they see who can do a 360. Lots of room is needed for this, because skiers get enthusiastic about spinning around.

Common Problems and Corrections

Problem	Description	Correction
Limited Leg Action	Skiers steer with just the foot, which provides little power to turn the ski.	Skiers rotate the entire leg to steer.
Excessive Torso Rotation	Skiers' upper bodies rotate to steer the skis, and shoulder swing may be strong.	Skiers try Helicopters and 180s again and let their feet do the work.

4 *Skiing Maneuvers*

Once skiers establish a solid foundation of skiing skills, the leader must blend the skills into various maneuvers. Children often don't notice the transition to these skiing moves, thinking the moves are just the same game. Children are usually willing to try something new, and maybe someone will think to ask later what it is called. But don't count on it!

Separating the practice of skills from techniques is misleading, because their development is interrelated. Skills are a great place to begin, because their simpler nature can make the learning process easier. Maneuvers are a more complex pattern of movements that involve the use of a combination of skills.

Experimentation with skills and maneuvers leads to a natural flow from one to the other. If practice of a particular move proceeds haltingly, young skiers benefit by a return to exercises that isolate the skills. This renewed practice of a simpler move lets skiers experience some success, and it helps to restore their confidence in themselves.

By increasing their repertoire of practice exercises for skills, instructors have more "tricks" in their big bag of activities to help new skiers who are having difficulty. More importantly, skiers see the components of a move more clearly, and they understand what makes it work. Also, a process for mastering the moves becomes apparent, and new skiers see a way to accomplish their goals. As a result, skiers are likely to attain the goal of efficient form more often.

I address maneuvers by two types of terrain—cross-country and downhill—rather than by Alpine or Nordic disciplines. Basic skiing mechanics cross the boundaries of each world, because some maneuvers are not exclusively the property of either Alpine or Nordic skiers. Basic downhill techniques are a good example, because both types of skiers need them to control their speed.

Obviously, Alpine skiers use downhill techniques more often than Nordic skiers. Cross-country techniques are more strongly the province of the free-heeled Nordic skiers. However, Alpine skiers' needs to handle flatter terrain and uphill climbs cannot be overlooked.

Let's look at more general definitions of each technique to identify the basic components applicable to both types of skiers. In certain cases, I further explain the techniques in terms of their Nordic or Alpine refinements to show some differences. Again, the intent is the use of simple language and descriptive images that leaders can use with children. More technical descriptions and analysis are readily available in other publications, and I make no attempt to re-create the technical language here.

Cross-Country Maneuvers

All skiers, whether Nordic or Alpine, encounter flat land and uphill climbs that force them to generate the power to move. Being able to move efficiently is the challenge, and learning effective techniques makes it easier to be a powerful skier on this terrain. Skiers will end up frustrated and fatigued if they fail to gain power with a minimum of effort.

Children often express boredom with flat terrain, and they will cast longing glances at nearby hills unless the instructor diverts their attention. But flat terrain plays an important role in learning to ski because it creates skier comfort. Eliminating the unnerving variable of ever-increasing speed is necessary until these skiers have the skills to control it. Exciting games and activities are an absolute necessity on flat terrain to capture the attention of children and lure them into necessary practice.

Getting Started

All young skiers need warm-up activities on flat terrain to get oriented to basic skiing moves. Nordic skiers can move easily, because their free heels allow them to play with freedom. Alpine skiers cannot ski as easily on flat terrain, but many stationary exercises, stretches, and short drills on flat terrain are appropriate to get oriented, as is some skiing on the flats. Warming up on flat terrain teaches skiers how to generate power for cruising over flatter trails.

Flatland programs offer the leader a good opportunity to assess the group's abilities and decide the nature of the activities. Children with balance problems may need more time on the flats and the gentlest of hills. Energetic gymnasts can handle the thrills of the hills sooner.

Flat terrain is a good place to take off skis and play boot games with little skiers who are struggling to control their skis. Getting used to the heavy boots is important for 2- and 3-year-olds. It's fun with this old familiar song: "You put your right foot in, you put your right foot out, you put your right foot in, and you shake it all about. . . ."

Climbing uphill requires efficiency of another sort, because it's frustrating to work hard and slide backward. Uphill maneuvers are used primarily by Nordic skiers, but Alpine skiers also need to climb hills to reach ski lifts (and to retrieve poles!). Familiarity with the techniques is important, and their practice is often useful to the learning of other downhill maneuvers. For instance, a herringbone to climb a hill is the basis for a skate turn later in the program.

The next section examines cross-country maneuvers and how they are used to generate power and speed. The necessary skills for each move are listed for easy reference. If a skier has difficulty with a movement, the leader should try to identify a specific skill that is causing the problem. When skiers choose practice activities that strengthen their skills, performance of the move usually follows more easily. The more complex moves have a longer list of skills, which helps to explain why skiers may have difficulty with some techniques more than others!

Double Poling

Double poling is using both arms simultaneously to give a powerful push forward. Skiers drop their upper bodies like a formal bow to a partner and push on their poles. The push occurs in an arc like a pendulum on a clock, with a downward swing and then a complete follow-through behind the skiers' bodies. The skiers return to an upright position to begin another round.

Children naturally use double poling and can generate enormous momentum with the right snow conditions. When the snow provides more resistance, skiers can use double poling on a slight downhill to increase speed. The maneuver is simple and is one of the easiest to learn, requiring only two skills—sliding and poling.

Nordic skiers use longer poles for a more powerful push. As a result, their poling is usually longer, slower, and more fluid, with a deeper bow from the waist. Alpine skiers use this maneuver briefly to get moving, but their short poles make it a shorter, faster move with a more upright body (Figure 4.1).

Skills: poling, sliding

Figure 4.1. Double poling.

Basic Exercises

O   *Bows.*   Skiers bend fully from the waist.

O   *Holding a Tray.*   Skiers extend their arms forward like they are holding a tray and swing them in an arc backward until they are as high as possible behind the skiers' bodies. Skiers touch their hands together.

O   *Arm Poling.*   Skiers use just their arms to pole, then contrast the motion with a full bow. Skiers get more power and longer glide with use of their entire upper bodies.

O   *Bobbing Birds.*   Skiers bend at the waist like feeding birds and push on their poles.

O   *Diving Platforms.*   Skiers stand on their skis as if ready to dive off a pool side (arms extended backward). They "dive" by swinging their arms forward and planting their poles for the push. Leaders should encourage aggressive diving! Children try so aggressively that they can fall forward, so they must be careful of the ski tips!

O   *Ski Jumper Lean.*   Skiers bend forward from their ankles into an airborne ski jumper's position, then double pole. Skiers lean as far as possible without lifting their heels off the skis. Here's another good exercise for aggressive leans! Skiers see how far they can glide. (A medium lean often creates the most balanced double pole.)

O   *Ski Jump Partners.*   Two skiers face each other with a wide stance. Their ski tips can overlap to get closer together. They start in a diving position and swing their arms forward to clap each other's hands. This meeting in the middle is a good exercise in trusting partners to be there! As skiers get comfortable, they can back farther apart and try again. They will have to lean into the middle more aggressively. Nordic skiers should keep their heels on their skis. Good practice of racing starts here for Alpine skiers (Figure 4.2)!

Figure 4.2. Ski Jump Partners encourages strong forward lean.

O *How Many Fingers?* Two partners work together, one skier ready to double pole and the other at the end of a skiing lane about 25 yards away. Every time the first skier double poles, the partner holds up a different number of fingers and the first skier must call out the number of fingers held. This encourages the first skier to keep looking down the track while poling (rather than at his or her feet).

Activities

△ *Longest Double Pole.* The leader establishes a starting line, and skiers line up with their tips several steps behind the line. Each skier takes a few shuffling steps, poles hard, and glides. Skiers mark the end spot and try it again for a personal best. They repeat on a gentle incline.

△ *Double Pole Subtraction.* The leader establishes a point-to-point course, and the skiers count the number of double poles between the points. They repeat and double pole fewer times. They keep trying until they reach their minimum limit.

△ *Stick Shifts.* Skiers with longer poles can experiment with first, second, and third "gear." First gear is a poling action with greatly bent arms, with lots of power to get the "cars" going. Second gear is poling with slightly extended arms, used once the skiers are moving. Third gear is poling with fully extended arms once the skiers are underway. Skiers pretend to be different kinds of cars, complete with sound effects! The leader can establish an obstacle course with slalom poles to mark the turns.

△ *Car Races.* Using a relatively straight-line obstacle course, skiers have to duck under "bridges" of various heights and pole through narrow "tunnels" of tight markers. Bridges can be made by planting two ski poles and hanging a third pole horizontally through the straps. A flatlands course usually requires some striding or skating between the double poling, which encourages nice transitions between the techniques.

Common Problems and Corrections

Problem	Description	Correction
Upright Body	A lack of "bowing" forces skiers to use only the weaker arm muscles without extra energy from the big muscles of the upper body.	Skiers contract their stomach muscles as if doing sit-ups and then bend over.
Frozen Bows	Skiers stay hunched over and use only their arms to pole.	Skiers practice up-and-down transitions, chanting "stand tall, bend over, stand tall." They find a landmark in the distance to look at each time they stand tall. They play How Many Fingers?
Flashing Headlights	Skiers swing their poles so the baskets point forward like headlights on a car.	Skiers practice positioning their poles like taillights, pointing behind the body!

Diagonal Stride

The diagonal stride is the most common Nordic move, because its action is similar to walking or running. It moves beyond walking, however, because it has the additional element of gliding. Skiers push off and glide to propel themselves forward. The free heels of Nordic skiers allow them to use this technique on all terrain (Figure 4.3).

The term *diagonal* refers to the opposite action of legs and arms that occurs naturally when people walk. This maneuver can be difficult to

Figure 4.3.   The diagonal stride.

learn if analyzed too long, because it involves a large list of required skills. Compare the number of required skills to those necessary in double poling, and it's evident that the diagonal stride is a more complex move. Skiers must let it flow naturally!

Walking on skis is the way to start. Toddlers can inch forward on the snow, simply getting used to these "long feet." Young children usually use a short, choppy stride at the outset, which propels them quickly and keeps them well balanced. Longer, stronger strides develop with practice and age, as older skiers feel more comfortable balancing on each leg. Eventually they are able to push off strongly and glide on each ski with their weight (i.e., their hips) farther forward. This more aggressive position helps to keep everything hurtling forward down the track! Children care very little about the picture-perfect diagonal stride. They just want to go, and if they're getting good traction, leaders should let them go!

Skiers also use the diagonal stride to climb hills; the steeper the terrain, the shorter the stride. Children can stomp or charge the hills with a quick, running stride. This aggressive action encourages them to stand straighter and to get better traction.

Skills: gliding on one ski, moving from ski to ski, pushing off, sliding, poling

Basic Exercises

O *Stride Varieties.* Skiers ski with short strides, then repeat with long, slow, or fast strides, discussing which feels best. They try jogging and running and repeat on a hill.

O *Airplanes.* Skiers swing the airplane (one of their skis) backward, swing it onto the runway, then step onto the ski as it lands. They repeat with the other ski. The airplanes taxi down the runway for a while (i.e., slide forward a bit), then skiers repeat the action with the other ski. Skiers will begin to take baby strides forward.

O *Crouching Lion.* In a stationary position, skiers spring from ski to ski.

O *Pogo Sticks.* Skiers "pop" from the ankles and move from ski to ski. Then they pop more subtly without as much spring, to remove excessive bobbing.

O *Backward Ski.* Skiers ski backward!

O *Pole Swings.* Skiers hold their poles at midpole and swing them while striding. Skiers keep the poles parallel to the skis, trying not to let the poles cross over the skis.

O *Groucho Marx.* Skiers exaggerate the bend at the ankles and slide from ski to ski with extremely bent ankles. Then they straighten just a bit!

O *Mae West Walk (or Madonna Walk).* Skiers swivel their hips forward with every stride.

O *Pull Toys.* Skiers pretend a string is attached to their navels and an imaginary partner is pulling the string forward down the track. Skiers keep their noses out over the imaginary string.

Activities

△ *Diagonal Stride Subtraction.* The leader establishes a point-to-point course; skiers count the number of strides between points and try to reduce the number of strides each time. Skiers experiment with pushing off harder or gliding longer.

△ *Dribbling.* Skiers place a small ball in the track in front of one ski tip. (The ball should be bigger than a tennis ball so the ski doesn't ride up over the ball!) Skiers push the ball down the track while doing the diagonal stride, then repeat with the other leg. This is great for developing a good step forward.

△ *Follow the Leader.*   Skiers ski with a partner and try to follow the partner's pace. They shouldn't try to go too fast! Skiers can synchronize the skiing, moving either side by side or with one following the other. This mimicry helps to get kids pushing off hard (to keep up) and gliding longer on their skis.

△ *Monster Walk.*   Skiers stomp uphill like a favorite monster.

△ *Charge!*   Skiers run uphill, looking toward the top and not at their feet.

△ *Short and Long.*   Skiers use short, choppy strides to climb hills, then use long, gliding strides. They discuss which is fastest.

△ *Toe Grabs.*   On an uphill climb, skiers slide their feet forward and grab the snow with their toes to gain traction.

△ *Tandem Dribbling.*   One skier pushes a ball down the field and passes it to a partner; they continue passing the ball. They widen the lane and pass the ball across greater distances.

Common Problems and Corrections

Problem	Description	Correction
Shuffling	Skiers are unable to balance on one ski.	Skiers practice Ski Scooters to improve balance and loosen up. They then strive for complete weight transfer from ski to ski.
Slipping Skis	Skiers may be pushing off when their feet are far apart.	Skiers position their feet side by side for strong push-off. They try to avoid bending from the waist, which interferes with good push-off.
Upright Stance	Skiers are stable, but their stance inhibits long glide and more aggressive skiing.	Skiers practice Ski Jumper Leans, leaning forward from their ankles and positioning their hips farther forward over the leading foot. Ski Scooters are also helpful (Figure 4.4).

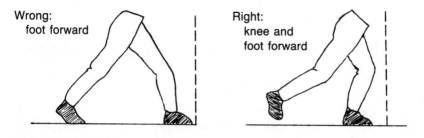

Figure 4.4. Shuffling is a common striding problem.

Problem	Description	Correction
Slapping Skis	The ski hits the snow behind the other foot rather than side by side.	An upright stance helps to create this slapping. Skiers practice the exercises that promote one-ski balance, such as Ski Scooters, and try moving from ski to ski with complete weight transfer.
Poor Timing	Skiers' arms and legs are uncoordinated.	Initially, taking the poles off and using a faster tempo to stride is helpful. Then skiers can develop a regular rhythm with the striding by concentrating on good weight transfer. Then skiers can try again with the poles, letting them drag along with natural arm swings. Skiers gradually apply more pressure on the poles, but focus on the arm swing to maintain good timing with the striding.

Skating (No Poles)

Skating is a powerful way to move across flat terrain, and it's a move that children who ice skate can identify readily like an old familiar friend. They are aware that racers use different skating maneuvers, and they consider it a hot technique!

Skiers usually skate on groomed, hard-packed snow. Skating is difficult in deep snow and more exciting on the faster conditions of packed snow.

Both Alpine and Nordic skiers skate with their skis in a V-shaped position. Young children call this "skiing like a duck," and they pretend to skate like ducks on an icy pond. Playing Mama Duck with a trail of baby ducks is an entertaining version of Follow the Leader.

To skate, skiers step forward onto a gliding ski and ride this flat ski as long as possible. As they prepare to step forward onto their other ski, they lean forward and gradually edge their gliding ski. Nordic skiers push off their skis and let their heels lift off the skis; Alpine skiers simply roll over their ski edges onto the other ski.

The determining factor in handling these skating moves is the skier's ability to balance on one ski at a time. Bringing the feet together and keeping a compact stance is helpful at the beginning of each skate. This "Mary Poppins" position with heels and knees together enables a skier to move forward nicely from a balanced position (Figure 4.5).

Figure 4.5. Keeping a compact stance is important at the beginning of each skate.

The arms should swing naturally throughout skating practice. As the skiers become more comfortable with their speed, they will begin to pump their arms like a speed skater.

Skills: gliding on one ski, moving from ski to ski, edging, pushing off

Basic Exercises

O   *Tin Soldier.*   In a stationary position, skiers rock from ski to ski like a tilting ice cube or tin soldier.

O   *Tin Soldier 2.*   Skiers rock from ski to ski. As skiers step onto each ski, they lift the other off the snow.

O   *Toe-Knee-Nose.*   As skiers rock onto each ski, they make sure their toes, knees, and noses are directly over the skis. They want a complete, balanced weight transfer.

O   *Skate Walk.*   Skiers walk in a skating position and step forward slightly each time. Then they step farther and farther forward. (Some gliding should result.)

O   *Solo Glides.*   Skiers push off and glide on a flat ski as far as possible. Then they try the other side, noticing any difference in the length of glide. (Skiers often have an ability to balance longer on one side.) They try to glide longer on each ski.

O   *Nibbles and Jaws.*   Skiers glide on a flat ski and roll it onto its inside edge to get a good bite against the snow. They can experiment with little bites (nibbles) and big bites (jaws) to see which feels better. (Jaws push skiers strongly, but some may not be able to ride out the momentum.)

O   *Flat Tracks.*   Skiers skate in softer snow and take a look at the track, discussing how far the widest portion of the track reaches (when the ski is flat) before the narrow part begins (when edging occurs). Skiers make more tracks and keep their skis flattened longer, which results in better glides.

O   *Speed Skating.*   Skiers swing their arms strongly like an ice skater while skating. They point their opposite fingers toward the tips of their gliding skis. Establishing a speed-skating oval course encourages the skiers to develop long, gradual turning skills. Skiers can try holding their hands behind their backs while skating, which results in less power and poor balance!

Activities

△   *Power Machines.*   The engine (one skier) stands behind the immovable object (another skier) and pushes the object along by pushing against his or her hips. The object uses the all-purpose sports stance to remain balanced, and the engine uses a skating stance to get good traction. Establishing a destination forces the engine to look around the object's body on alternate sides and encourages solid weight transfer from ski to ski (Figure 4.6).

Figure 4.6. Power Machines develops controlled skating on flat terrain.

△ *Ape Skating.*   While skating, skiers sweep their hands below their knees like gorillas.

△ *Zipper Swivel.*   Skiers line up their jacket zippers with their skating skis, which should create Toe-Knee-Nose alignment.

△ *Double Dribbling.*   Skiers practice dribbling a ball down a lane. They try to push the ball from one skating ski to the other one without the ball bouncing over the skis. Then two skiers skate next to each other. One dribbles the ball and then passes it to the other person and they continue passing the ball while traveling down the field. They repeat the exercise and widen the distance between each other (Figure 4.7).

△ *Slalom Course.*   Skiers use a straight-line course to skate around the poles (quicker turns) and then an offset course (more skating mixed with turns). They try to skate only once between each pole. The offset course develops longer gliding on one ski.

Figure 4.7. Double Dribbling provides skating practice.

Common Problems and Corrections

Problem	Description	Correction
Short Glide	Skiers are unable to balance on one leg. Their glide develops a fast tempo that gets out of control.	Skiers practice more one-ski exercises like Ski Scooters and Toe Lifts.
Straddles	Again, balance is the problem. Skiers keep their weight between their skis and won't commit fully to each ski.	Skiers practice the Mary Poppins and Toe-Knee-Nose positions. They click the heels together before skating onto the new ski.
Skidding Out and Splits	Skiers use improper edging.	Skiers practice biting the inside edges of their skis into the snow to prevent the skis from sliding sideways. Nibbles and Jaws is a good exercise for edge control.

Problem	Description	Correction
Upright Stance		Skiers move their hips farther forward by bending at the ankle and by moving their hips over their feet. Then they step farther forward for more aggressive skating and gamble with their bodies being "out there" over the skis!

Sidestepping

Sidestepping is one of the most basic moves because it offers excellent control over the skis. All skiers can use sidestepping to climb uphill and if necessary to descend a hill safely (Figure 4.8).

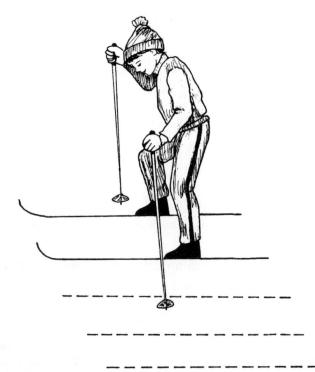

Figure 4.8. Sidestepping is a sturdy way to climb uphill.

To sidestep, skiers lift one ski sideways across the snow and then bring the other ski next to it in a parallel position. On a hill, skiers begin with their skis across the incline perpendicular to the fall line (the imaginary line that follows the steepest angle of the slope). The skis are edged depending upon the steepness of the hill. The steeper the hill, the greater the edging to prevent the skis from skidding out (Figure 4.9).

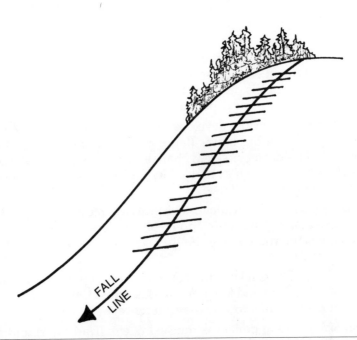

Figure 4.9. Keeping the skis perpendicular to the fall line is important when sidestepping.

When exploring unfamiliar trails, skiers can find themselves at the top of a hill that is beyond their abilities. Sidestepping can be extremely useful in handling the steepest part of the hill until skiers reach a part they can ski using other techniques. Even expert skiers find it a handy option.

Skills: moving from ski to ski, edging

Basic Exercises

O   *Thousand Steps.*   Skiers experiment with many little sidesteps rather than big ones. This feels better for the youngest children especially.

O   *Changing Directions*.   A group of skiers sidestep in one direction, then the leader calls a change in direction, speeding up the changes to develop quick reflexes. The leader acts like a traffic officer and points in different directions. Skiers are forced to look up and away from their skis to follow the signals.

O   *Ridges and Bridges*.   The leader creates a path with ridges of snow to step over, bridges of poles to duck under, and a big mountain to climb at the end. Skiers sidestep along the obstacle course.

Activities

△   *Catch Your Neighbor*.   A group of skiers sidestep in a big circle with about 10 feet between each person. They start slow, step a little faster, and then the leader calls out "catch your neighbor." Skiers sidestep very quickly to tag the next person.

△   *Chorus Line*.   The leader develops a line dance with skiers standing side by side and holding hands (large groups or small ones). After a set number of sidesteps, skiers change directions. They later add various stage moves, such as bows, kicks, dips, or splits. The skiers can hum or sing as they dance.

△   *Climb the Ladder*.   The leader establishes two tracks heading uphill. Skiers sidestep along the route and create ladders in the snow. The leader changes the route along the way so skiers traverse and climb a different ladder.

△   *Sideslipping*.   Skiers release their ski edges and slip downhill, biting with the edges to stop and keeping the skis across the hill. Skiers try big bites and little ones to test the difference!

△   *Blind Skiing*.   One person is the seeing eye (lead skier) and the other is a blind skier (follower who closes his or her eyes). They hold hands side by side, and the seeing eye leads up the hill, using sidestepping, traversing forward, and traversing backward. This activity keeps skiers from looking at their feet and encourages them to feel the changes in terrain.

△   *Team Tug-of-War*.   The leader establishes two teams and leaves about 10 feet between skiers as they grab the rope. (The leader should provide a long rope so skiers can fall without hitting others!) Each team tries to pull the other team across the dividing line drawn in the snow. The leader should use flat terrain for this game. This game develops great aggressive edging and balancing on one leg!

Common Problems and Corrections

Problem	Description	Correction
Crossed Skis	Skiers can't keep their skis parallel.	Skiers take smaller steps and go slowly until they can place skis side by side.
Looking Down	Skiers look at their skis to make sure they're parallel.	Skiers practice Thousand Steps and Changing Directions with closed eyes; "blind skiing" (eyes closed) lets the skiers feel what their feet are doing.
Limited Fall Line Awareness	Skiers slide down-hill when they are no longer perpen-dicular to the fall line.	Skiers take small steps and test each one. They transfer a little weight to feel the security before full commitment.

Herringbone

The herringbone is the uphill version of "walking like a duck." Both Alpine and Nordic skiers use this technique to climb. The skiers place their skis in the V-shaped position and step up the hill. The skis are edged against the snow to prevent sliding backward. The skiers use their poles in the normal walking rhythm of the diagonal stride (Figure 4.10).

The action is more than simply rocking from ski to ski, which causes skiers to trip over their ski tails; skiers must step forward to move uphill and step free of the other ski.

Skiers also need to stand tall like giants and look at the top of the hill. This action keeps the body weight stacked evenly over the middle of the skis. If skiers bend over, they lose proper edging and balance over the skis, and they begin to slide downhill.

The basic herringbone can be modified in several ways. On easy terrain, a half-V position can be an effective and fast way to move

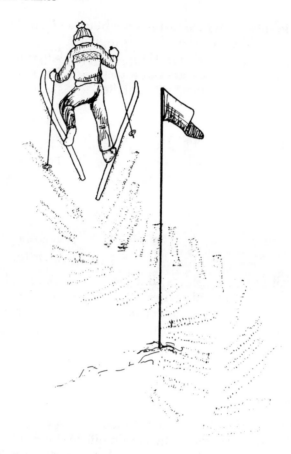

Figure 4.10. Herringbone.

uphill. On steeper terrain, this half herringbone can be used when climbing a hill on a diagonal rather than straight up.

The gliding herringbone is another variation, also known as *diagonal V* in Nordic skiing. As skiers step uphill, they can push off the edged ski and glide onto the new ski. The technique becomes more fluid and fewer moves are required.

> *Skills: moving from ski to ski, edging, pushing off, poling, gliding on one ski (gliding herringbone)*

Basic Exercises

O   Skiers repeat any of the general skating exercises.

O   *Half Herringbone.*   Skiers use a half-V position and move up the hill on a diagonal angle. This takes longer than the herringbone but is easier. Skiers now try the half-V straight up a hill. If slipping occurs, they change to the full V of the herringbone.

O *Tacking.* Skiers tack like a sailboat to climb uphill and create a zigzagged path. This is a nice way to handle a steeper hill.

Activities

△ *Duck, Duck, Goose.* Skiers line up at the bottom of a hill facing uphill. Each skier extends a hand backward over the tails of the skis. One person shuffles behind the skiers (downhill side), slapping their hands and saying "duck, duck, duck" and finally slaps a hand while saying "goose." The goose begins to herringbone uphill, while the person who slapped the goose's hand turns around, squeezes through the vacant spot, and chases the goose uphill. Throwing a hat or mitten is the safest way to tag a goose.

△ *Traffic Patterns.* A group of skiers tack like sailboats to climb a hill in follow-the-leader fashion. Then, two groups begin at opposite corners and climb uphill on a diagonal route. The skiers meet at the middle of the X and dart around each other to keep climbing. Great patterns emerge, as does an awareness of other skiers on the hill.

△ *Obstacle Courses.* The leader lays flagging or rope on the hill in V-shaped patterns that skiers must step up and over as they climb uphill. Then the leader adds several sections with small and large spaces between the Vs, between which skiers can take only one step. They have to change the size of their steps and stay in control.

△ *Simon Says.* Skiers play this old favorite on the hill with the leader at the top. The instructions to the group can be, "Simon says take a little step, take a big step, step sideways, charge the hill" and so on.

△ *Herringbone Corridor 1.* The leader establishes an avenue that changes in width, marking it with tracks in the snow or two ropes. An hourglass or funnel figure is effective in making skiers change from a wide herringbone to a narrow one when they climb uphill.

△ *Herringbone Corridor 2.* The leader establishes an avenue about 1 foot wider than a herringbone. Skiers glide on each ski until the ski tip touches the edge of the corridor. The leader widens the corridor as skiers improve their glide.

△ *Stepping Stones.* The leader measures the length of each skier's uphill step on a gliding herringbone. Skiers try to step farther and farther uphill on repeated drills. They begin on a gentle uphill then move to steeper terrain.

△ *Mirror Images.* Two skiers play follow the leader with gliding herringbones. If the leader is a stronger skier, the follower gets great practice with timing and good glide. They switch roles and repeat.

Common Problems and Corrections

Problem	Description	Correction
Slipping Downhill	Skiers are bent over.	Skiers stand tall, look at the top of the hill, and step from ski to ski in place. They let their skis roll onto the inside edge when stepping off, then they step forward.
Clicking Tails	Skiers step sideways rather than forward.	Skiers try to move up the hill!
Little Glide (on a gliding herringbone)	Skiers straddle the snow and rock between their skis.	They stand completely on each ski with a good Toe-Knee-Nose position. They try to flatten their skis longer and avoid edging too soon. Skiers can return to the flats or a gentler hill to practice. They try to add power to their glide.

Kick Double Pole

This Nordic maneuver is also known as a one-step double pole, and it combines double poling with a push of the leg. When double poling isn't moving a skier quickly enough, the kick double pole adds extra zip. It is effective on flat terrain and is a good transition to a downhill run (Figure 4.11).

Picture the beginning of double poling, when a skier's arms are extended forward for the poling. At this point, the skier can let one leg rise from the ground as a counterbalance to the extended arms. The skier holds his or her arms out forward, with the leg extended

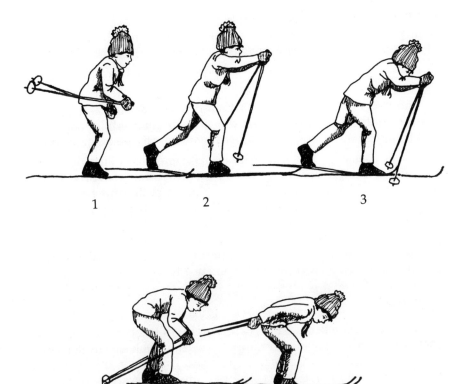

1   2   3

4   5

Figure 4.11. Kick double pole.

toward the rear. As the poles push against the snow, the extended leg drives forward. Both arms and leg meet at the skier's body. The arms swing backward to complete the poling, and the skier glides on both legs. It's wise to alternate the legs to eliminate fatigue, but it's easier to isolate each side in initial practice.

During double poling, many skiers often let one ski slide backward slightly for better balance, and children use this effect naturally to get more power. The kick double pole is difficult for children to think about; leaders should let it happen naturally.

Skills: sliding, poling, balancing on one leg, moving from ski to ski, push-off

Basic Exercises

O   Skiers repeat double poling exercises.

O   *Scissors Kick*.   Skiers lean forward from their ankles and lean on their poles for balance. Skiers let one ski lift slightly backward and use a scissors kick to bring it beside the other ski. They alternate sides.

O   *Slow and Fast Scissors*.   Skiers experiment with the difference between slow and fast scissor kicks. Fast scissors are crisp and powerful.

O   *Airplane Landings*.   Skiers use their poles for balance and lean forward from their ankles. They let the airplane (one ski) lift backward a little higher and swing it onto the runway next to the other airplane.

O   *Going Bananas*.   This stationary exercise emphasizes timing. Skiers assume an extended or open stance with arms stretched forward and one leg lifted backward slightly. They bring both arms back to the body by double poling and swinging the leg forward (a closed stance). The leader can use a key word like "banana" every time the skiers assume the extended position or can use words such as "open" and "closed." These words work as a timing device. The leader should shout the buzzword while skiers practice the technique.

Activities

△   *Tandem Ski Jumpers*.   This is an exercise in trust! Two skiers face each other with their skis overlapping (without poles). The skiers assume an extended stance, leaning forward from their ankles toward each other. Their palms press together, and each skier extends a leg rearward. (To eliminate confusion, the leader specifies the right or left leg.) Skiers mimic the double pole action and swing their legs forward at the same time (the closed stance). Then they swing their legs to the extended stance again. They move farther apart and try it again. They repeat with the other leg, eventually practicing while alternating the legs that are extended.

△   *Longest Kick Double Pole*.   The leader establishes a starting line. Skiers stride to the line and use a kick double pole as hard as they can (it happens naturally). They mark the spot where their glide ends and try for a personal best.

△   *Longest Kick Double Pole 2*.   The leader establishes a starting line on the lip of a hill. Skiers repeat the activity. Children often drop right into a tuck to go farther.

Common Problems and Corrections

Problem	Description	Correction
Bent Body	Skiers hinge from the waist rather than assuming the classic ski jumper's lean.	Skiers move their hips forward over their toes, so far that the wrinkles in their clothing are smoothed out. Skiers must be brave! One leg should lift rearward in a natural fashion. The more aggressive the lean in front, the higher the leg lift in the rear should be to counterbalance.
Poor Timing	The extended leg seems useless and fails to swing toward the body in time with the arms.	Skiers use Going Bananas to memorize the synchronized actions.
Upright Body	The double poling is all arms.	Skiers return to pure double poling for a while and practice good up-and-down movement of the upper body for better power. Then they return to the kick double pole.

Marathon Skate

Skiers use the marathon skate, in which double poling is combined with skating, to get additional power in groomed tracks. The extra push comes from a half-skate action.

Imagine skiers who are beginning to double pole. They extend their arms forward to plant the poles and at the same time lift one ski from the track and place it at an angle to the track and against the snow (so that the tails cross and the skis form a half-V shape). As skiers begin to pole, they step forward onto this skating leg and simultaneously glide on it (Figure 4.12).

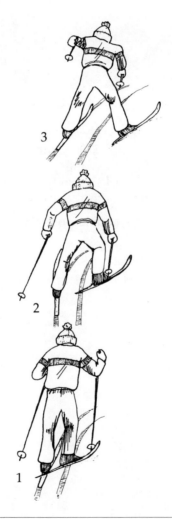

Figure 4.12. Marathon skate.

As the poling extends behind the body, skiers still glide on the skating skis. The skating ski is flatter for better glide and is edged at the end to get the skiers back to a good poling stance. When their arms swing forward, the skiers shift their weight onto the skis in the track.

A crucial element in effective marathon skating is transferring weight completely from the ski in the track to the angled ski. Many skiers keep their weight completely on the tracked ski and obtain little power from the skating ski.

The technique resembles the kick double pole and the V1 in the timing. In all three techniques, every double poling action requires one extra push of some kind.

Adolescents usually have success with marathon skating because they can synchronize the various components. Young children, unless they are very coordinated, find this type of skating too complex.

Skills: sliding, gliding on one leg, moving from ski to ski, poling, edging, pushing off

Basic Exercises

O   Skiers repeat basic double poling exercises.

O   *Half-V's.* Skiers use a half-V position in tracks and rock from their tracked ski to the angled or skating ski. They let the tracked ski lift until it clicks against the skating ski.

O   *Blind Half-V's.* Skiers step into the half-V position with closed eyes and feel whether the skating foot is ahead of the tracked foot.

O   *Scooters (without poles).* Skiers use the skating ski to push down the track. They keep their weight on the tracked ski first, then rock onto the skating ski and back to the tracked one.

Activities

△   *Small and Large V's.* Skiers experiment with different angles of the half-Vs when marathon skating, discussing which one gives a better push from a complete stop (large) and which one keeps a skier moving better (smaller).

△   *Switching Tracks.* Skiers slide onto the skating ski and ride it across the median strip to the next tracks. They play Follow the Leader (Figure 4.13).

△   *Line Dances.* Three skiers line up in the same track. The lead skier sets the pace and the group mimics it so that everyone marathon skates at the same time. This improves timing for those having difficulties. Lead skier peels off by skating into another track, and the next person becomes the lead skier.

Figure 4.13. Playing follow the leader and preparing to switch tracks.

△ *Alternating Line Dances.* Skiers switch tracks during the line dance. The lead skier can spice up the changes and make them quick ones.

Common Problems and Corrections

Problem	Description	Correction
No Weight Transfer (to the skating ski)	Skiers have less power because they don't step completely onto the skating ski.	Skiers emphasize the weight transfer by skating onto the angled ski and slightly lifting the ski in the track.
Skating Ski Drags Behind	Skiers step sideways onto the skating ski.	Skiers step forward onto the skating ski and glide diagonally forward on it.
Skating Ski Skids Out	Skiers fail to edge the skating ski when they push off it to return to the sliding ski.	Skiers edge the ski slightly and make sure weight has been transferred to it before pushing off.

V1

V1 is an effective skating maneuver used by Nordic skiers on uphills and flats. It combines skating with double poling for extra power. V1 is skating with double poling on one side only; for every two skating steps, the skier double poles once.

V1 is part of the new skating techniques that have changed Nordic skiing. Each maneuver gains its name from the symmetrical V shape created by the skis, and the number associated with the name refers to the type of poling.

In V1, the skier has a *power side*, on which the double poling occurs, and a *free glide side*, where no poling occurs. The skier poles and steps onto the power side simultaneously. The timing of poling and stepping is crucial, and learning the basic moves without skis can be helpful (Figure 4.14).

Figure 4.14.   The skiers synchronize the poling and skating in V1.

V1 is appropriate for children who can use each leg independently in skiing and who have good timing between poling and body actions. Children who shuffle excessively or use their poles as crutches will find V1 skating too frustrating.

Children between 8 and 9 years of age can use V1 beautifully and can actually improve their diagonal striding. The skating improves their ability to glide one each leg, which in turn makes them more efficient striders.

Skills: gliding on one ski, moving from ski to ski, edging, pushing off, poling

Basic Exercises

O   Skiers repeat any of the basic skating exercises.

O   *Toe-Knee-Nose Revisited.*   Skiers line up their toes, knees, and noses over one of their skis for the proper body position and frame the ski with extended arms. They swivel their bodies to their other ski and frame the other ski with their arms. They repeat with closed eyes to feel a rhythmic, swiveling action, then stop when each ski feels framed and check to make sure it is.

O   *Power Slaps (without poles).*   Skiers choose a ski to be the power side. They step onto the ski and simultaneously slap the leg of the power ski. The leader can use a key word like "bang" or "pole" to encourage good timing. Slapping the legs brings the upper body over the power ski. Skiers then move to the free glide side without using a key word. They practice this exercise in place and then repeat it by taking small steps forward.

O   *Hang Five.*   Skiers stand on V-shaped skis, reach forward with their arms, and angle their poles behind their feet. Skiers swing their hands over to the power side until they frame the ski. (The torso should rotate until it's over the skis also.) The arms are now angled to one side with a higher outside hand and a lower inside hand. Skiers hang off the higher hand (power side) and let the lower hand (free glide side) cross their bodies. They change the power side and repeat, noticing whether one side feels more comfortable.

O   *Pole Chant (without skis but with poles).*   Skiers choose a power side. They step and pole simultaneously over the power side, saying "pole" when both ski and pole hit the snow. They move to the free glide side (saying nothing) and back to the power side. They develop a chanting rhythm. Skiers practice this exercise in place before taking steps forward. After the skiers establish timing, the leader should check to see if the poling frames the skis.

O   *Pole Chant (with skis).*   Skiers repeat the drill with skis. Skiers should take small steps when they begin to move, to control their balance. They should concentrate on timing more than gliding.

O   *Dorothy of Oz.*   Skiers initially try this in place. They click their heels together at the completion of each skating step, bringing the heel completely over to the other foot to encourage a compact stance and to avoid the splits! Then they try it while moving. Skiers may find they can click better on one side than the other. They should keep practicing on the weaker side.

O   *Around the World.*   This poling exercise is better practiced in place initially. Skiers' arms simulate a circular motion like an around-the-world stretching exercise. Skiers double pole over the power side and extend their arms behind them. They return their poles to the free glide side until their arms are extended and then move the poles across to the power side. The arms complete a somewhat triangular around-the-world route, but they help to keep skiers balanced over each ski.

Activities

△ *Take a Walk on the Glide Side.* The intent is to glide as far as possible on the free glide side. Skiers pole each time along a boundary—the edge of a wide trail or practice area—and glide into the field or trail each time. They try to glide farther and farther.

△ *Synchronized Skiing.* One skier skis behind a partner and synchronizes their poling. The skier tries to match the partner's glide.

Common Problems and Corrections

Problem	Description	Correction
Poor Timing	The poling and skating are not synchronized.	Skiers slow down and use Pole Chants to synchronize the poling and skating. The leader shouts the key word.
Short Glide	Skiers have poor one-ski balance and often rock quickly from ski to ski.	Skiers return to one-ski exercises like Ski Scooters to improve balance. Skiers concentrate on sliding on a flat ski rather than edging too soon.
Centered Body	The body straddles the V rather than swiveling over each ski. The glide is shortened, and the action is shorter and more choppy.	Skiers return to Toe-Knee-Nose exercises to move the body completely over each ski.
Little Upper Body Use	A lack of bowing, or up-and-down action, limits a skier's power.	Skiers review efficient double poling, with which the torso provides the thrust.

V2

V2 is a powerful skating move used by Nordic skiers, although Alpine skiers will find its motion familiar. It combines skating with double poling for extra power and allows skiers to accelerate on flat terrain. It's also a good transition move as skiers come over the lip of a hill or begin a descent.

The skier double poles over each ski in V2; for every complete skating action (or V), the skier glides twice and poles twice. This action creates a stronger form of skating than V1 (poling only once for every two glides). The timing on the poling is also important for increased speed. The poling occurs after the skier steps onto the gliding ski . The staggered timing creates momentum more consistently throughout the maneuver (Figure 4.15).

Figure 4.15. As poling approaches the body in V2, the skier skates onto the other ski.

Alpine skiers use a similar move when a racer leaves the starting gate or a recreational skier skates to the lift. Many Alpine skiers who try Nordic skiing discover that the skating techniques become comfortable quickly.

V2 is a fast maneuver and one that children can learn easily. They often use it instinctively to race across an open space. Keeping up with the speed may be a problem at the outset, when one-ski balance can be wobbly. The timing of the poling may come and go for some young skiers. By junior high school, skiers are capable of extremely smooth racing technique.

The power skiers can achieve with V2 on flat terrain challenges children to see how far they can climb a hill. It's amazing how high these young powerhouses can get before they bail out and change to another technique.

Skills: gliding on one ski, moving from ski to ski, poling, edging, pushing off

Basic Exercises

O   Skiers use any of the basic skating exercises.

O   *Power Pushes.*   Two skiers face each other with their skis in a V shape. They lean into each other until their inside shoulders touch, and then they push against each other. They can move apart slightly and repeat the pushing. This "trust" exercise gives each skier a chance to try an aggressive forward lean without falling over (Figure 4.16).

Figure 4.16.   Power Pushes encourage good forward lean.

○ *Step and Pole 1.* This simple stationary exercise reinforces staggered V2 timing. Skiers stand with skis parallel. They step one ski out to a V and double pole over that ski (mock the action without digging in the poles). They step the other ski out to a V and then double pole over it. If they can't balance on one foot, they can place the other ski alongside the first. Skiers keep repeating the moves until their timing is correct.

○ *Step and Pole 2.* This stationary exercise refines timing. Skiers step onto one ski then mimic the double poling action over the ski. As their hands approach their bodies, skiers step onto their other ski and balance on it. After the arms swing backward completely, they return to a position over the ski that the skiers are standing on. Skiers double pole over this new ski and as their hands reach their bodies step onto the other ski. Skiers repeat the actions until the timing is smooth.

Activities

△ *Double Pole, Double Pole.* This moving exercise is an intermediate step toward a real V2! Skiers glide on two skis (skating on one ski can be hard at first) and concentrate on the timing. Skiers begin with double poling. As their hands approach their bodies, skiers step off diagonally (mimicking the basic V shape) and glide onto both skis. Skiers double pole again (over the gliding skis) and step in the other direction as their hands approach their bodies. Once the timing feels solid, skiers repeat the exercise while gliding onto one ski. That's V2!

△ *The Improved Double Pole, Double Pole.* This exercise reinforces good double poling and longer glide with the above drill. The double poling must be complete, with the arms extending fully behind the skiers. The skiers can bring the hands together behind the body to make sure! Otherwise, the skiers can rush the move and develop poor timing.

△ *V2 Corridor.* The leader establishes a narrow corridor with good boundaries (between poles or clothing). Skiers practice the V2 down the corridor. Skiers must reach each boundary before skating in the other direction. The leader gradually increases the width for skating farther. Skiers with balance problems can begin with the Double Pole, Double Pole drill along this corridor. Once they have established a rhythm, they can change into V2.

Common Problems and Corrections

Problem	Description	Correction
Poor Balance	The ability to slide on one side is limited.	Skiers repeat Ski Scooter exercises.

Problem	Description	Correction
Poor Timing	The poling and skating is not staggered consistently.	Skiers practice stationary exercises to isolate the Step-and-Pole sequence.
Stepping (rather than skating)	Skiers step down on their skating skis (sending their energy into the ground).	They should slide onto the skis (and send their energy forward). Skiers scuff the skis on the snow like scraping bubblegum off the bottom.

Downhill Maneuvers

Most children love hills and search for the ones that offer an exciting ride—the steeper and bumpier the better. Children rarely fear speed and are often willing to tackle descents beyond their abilities.

Laying a firm foundation of skills on flat or gentle terrain is important so skiers can bring well-honed tricks to the hills. An exciting series of games and activities gives children ample opportunity to learn to control their speed (generated by their own exuberance), and it teaches them basic moves before they control a different kind of speed (generated by the steepness of the hill).

A good challenge is encouraging older children to move beyond "strafing runs" and to begin to "play" the hill. Strafing runs are fast, straight descents to the bottom of a hill. The instructor can call for a dash of flash, a sprinkling of exciting moves between the speedy descents, by challenging skiers to perform as many different moves as possible in a given run, to dampen their speed when necessary and to let the power explode with other moves. With this method skiers become more versatile in the long run, and their safety is enhanced as well.

Downhill maneuvers are predominantly the domain of Alpine skiers, who focus on their descents. They experiment with a great variety of turning techniques to handle many different trails. Nordic skiers need the downhill moves because there is great reward in descending what has just been climbed. But the downhills are not the primary focus of cross-country skiing.

The instructor can introduce many downhill moves more safely by eliminating poles. Falling is less hazardous, and skiers will learn to stand up properly without relying on their crutches. The instructor can reintroduce poles after wedge turns, when skiers are comfortable with turning.

These general guidelines can be helpful in choosing a progression of activities.

- Warming-up: boot games, one-ski activities
- Descending hills: straight run, gliding wedge (snowplow)
- Controlling speed: braking wedge
- Turning: wedge turns, christies, parallel turns, telemark turns
- Increasing speed: skate turns

Straight Run

The place to begin learning downhill maneuvers is a straight run on a gentle hill with a flat "landing zone" at the bottom. Skiers can simply cruise to a stop without having to apply the brakes. Developing balance and comfort is crucial at the outset, and a variety of straight runs can ease the learning of other maneuvers.

For the straight run, skiers slide downhill in the all-purpose sports stance, standing flat-footed on the skis, with legs relaxed and flexed at the knees and ankles and hands in front of the body. Skiers experiment with lots of departures from the basic stance, such as balancing on one ski or rocking from ski to ski! (Figure 4.17).

Skills: sliding, balancing on one leg, moving from ski to ski

Figure 4.17.   Straight run.

Basic Exercises

O *Horse Races.*   Skiers kneel on their skis, hold the tips, and slide downhill. (This is good for Nordic skiers with poor balance or those who are afraid of falling.) Skiers can race each other to the finish line at the bottom.

O *Slump-O-Matic.*   Skiers relax their muscles and slump into the all-purpose sports stance before sliding down the hill.

O *Quiet Hands.*   Skiers slide with their hands on their thighs, then on their hips.

O *Chair Sitting.*   Skiers drop their bodies slightly as if sitting on the edge of a chair, then slide.

O *Giants and Midgets.*   Skiers stand tall with legs extended, then crouch small. A midway position should feel more balanced (Figure 4.18).

Figure 4.18. Giants and Midgets varies the basic stance from high to low.

O   *Touch the Sky.*   Skiers reach toward the sky, then reach for the ground, while sliding.

O   *Jack-in-the-Box.*   Skiers pop up and down while sliding

O   *Walk on the Wild Side.*   Skiers "walk" downhill, letting their feet slide forward.

O   *Ice Cubes.*   Skiers rock from ski to ski while sliding.

O   *One-Legged Gliding.*   Skiers stand on one of their skis, then on the other one, while sliding.

O   *Knee Grabs.*   Skiers crouch down and hold their knees while sliding.

O   *Birdland.*   Skiers flap like birds, land smoothly, and tuck in their wings. They soar like eagles, flap like ducks, and chirp like sparrows while sliding.

O   *Step-Overs.*   Skiers take a straight run, then step to the side, one foot at a time. They step over an obstacle such as a hat.

O   *The Rabbit.*   Skiers hop gently while sliding.

O   *Lion-Hearted.*   Skiers leap and pounce while sliding.

O   *Squirt Power.*   Skiers sit back on their skis while sliding.

O   *Tippy-Toes.*   Skiers press forward on the tips of their skis while sliding. (The Nordic skiers may topple forward! Press lightly!)

O   *Yellow Brick Road.*   Skiers ski stiffly like the tin soldier or ski loosely like the scarecrow.

Activities

△   *Tunnels.*   Skiers ski under an arch of poles. They can also try to balance an object on a tray (Figure 4.19).

△   *The Limbo.*   Skiers ski under a pole that is lowered after each round. Skiers should duck forward rather than lean backward. The person who can ski under the lowest point wins!

△   *Group Sliding.*   Skiers hold hands with a partner or a small group. They must be ready to let go if someone starts to fall!

△   *Tandem Jack-in-the-Boxes.*   Skiers ski side by side in pairs. One person is Jack and the other matches Jack's pops.

△   *Obstacle Course.*   Long, gradual hills are great for many imaginative obstacles. Skiers ski through a teepee (crossed poles), over a brook (a rope), along the brook's edge, and over the brook again.

Figure 4.19. Tunnels are great obstacle courses.

Common Problems and Corrections

Problem	Description	Correction
Stiff Posture	Skis chatter and cross when skiers' legs are very stiff.	Skiers use the Slump-O-Matic to relax. If the hill is too steep for comfort, skiers should try a gentler slope or traverse the hill.

Problem	Description	Correction
Hinging	Skiers bend forward, preventing them from reacting to changes in terrain.	Skiers mimic a butler with good posture and hold a tray in front.
Sitting Back	Skiers lean against the back of their boots, weight on their heels.	Skiers roll their weight toward the balls of their feet. They stand flatfooted and press their shins against their boot tongue. They act like a Jack-in-the-box.

Wedge (Snowplow)

The wedge or snowplow is one of the fundamental downhill techniques. Used for controlling speed or stopping, it is a necessary tool for beginners. Skiers can learn other downhill techniques from this basic position.

The skis are simultaneously steered into an A position so that the tips point together and the tails are wide apart. Each angled ski is a mirror image of the other as they brush across the snow. The width of the angle varies; a wide wedge is very stable, while a narrow wedge enables a skier to make changes quickly (particularly a transition to a turn).

Skiers use two types of wedges: gliding and braking. In the gliding wedge, the skis lie relatively flat to the snow and slide over it easily with less edging. The wedge is usually narrower. In the braking wedge, the skis are edged more strongly and actually "plow" up snow. The wedge is usually wider (Figure 4.20).

Good wedge practice begins on flat terrain, where skiers learn the basic position without worrying about speed. Lots of stationary exercises help skiers memorize positions. Children who play "pie" or "pizza" games with the wedge develop such comfort that they will automatically stop themselves at the end of straight runs.

Children who have problems with the wedge benefit by having the leader ski backward and hold their ski tips. This directs the skis properly so the skiers can develop a good feel for the position.

Cross-country skiers can use half-wedges in the tracks to slow their speed; this means one ski stays in the track and the other is angled

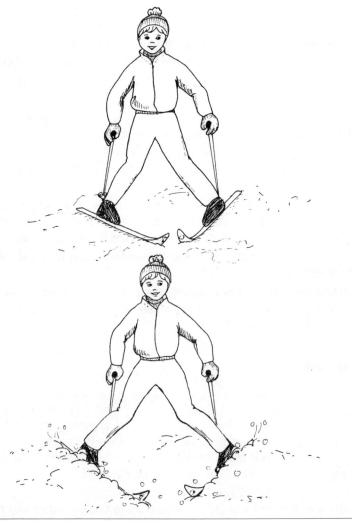

Figure 4.20. Gliding and braking wedges.

in the wedge. By the time skiers reach the hills, they know the feel of an angled, braking ski.

Skills: sliding, steering, edging, skidding

Basic Exercises

O *Brushes.* Skiers skid one ski into position by brushing the snow. Skiers brush up a ridge of snow, then brush with the other ski. They sweep strongly by steering with their big toes.

O   *Hopping A's.*   Skiers rise up and hop into an A shape.

O   *Skidding A's.*   Skiers skid both skis into the A shape.

O   *Blind Wedges.*   Skiers sink into the wedge with closed eyes.

O   *Press the Basketball.*   Skiers sink into the wedge with imaginary basketballs between their knees.

O   *Tall, Small.*   Skiers hop from narrow to wide wedges. They discuss which position makes them taller or smaller.

O   *Walking Wedges.*   Skiers use short steps to "walk out" into a narrow wedge, then a wide wedge. They walk back into a parallel position.

O   *Stop Sign.*   Skiers finish a straight run with a wedge. The leader places a marker at a point where the skiers will stop. Later, the leader moves the marker farther up the hill for a quicker stop.

O   *Creep Like a Snail.*   Skiers use a wide wedge to ski slowly. They try creeping down the hill.

O   *Squeeze Plays.*   Skiers mix wide and narrow wedges for variable speed control. They ski between sets of markers that are alternately close and far apart.

Activities

△   *Snowplow Trains.*   One skier is the plow and another skier is the engine (with or without skis). The engine pushes the plow across flat terrain. The plow can brake and make the engine work harder. Skiers can have train races or pretend to plow the city streets along an established route. This is great for 9- and 10-year-old children who are fearful of the hills. It makes both legs work equally!

△   *Pie Tag (or Pizza Tag).*   The leader establishes a playing field with boundaries. One skier is "it" and tries to tag the other skiers. Skiers are safe if they sink into a wedge and call out their favorite pie (or pizza). Five-year-olds love this!

△   *Tandem Tug-of-War.*   Two skiers stand side by side, facing in opposite directions. They stand in wedge positions and hold inside hands. They try to pull each other off balance with pulls, lunges, and fakes. This requires great aggressive edging. They change sides to exercise their other legs.

△   *Numbered Pies.*   The leader assigns numbers 1 through 5 to pie shapes that vary respectively from narrow to wide. Number 5 is a complete stop! The leader calls out a number as skiers descend, and they sink into the right shape. Skiers can then count from 1 to 5 as they descend and can change their wedges as they call out each number.

△ *Smooth Tracks.* Skiers look at their wedge tracks and see if they are the same for each ski. If one digs in too much, the skier must smooth it out by flattening the ski.

△ *Slowest Snowplow Races.* On "go," the entire group begins to snowplow downhill as slowly as possible without stopping. The trick is to keep moving. The slowest person wins!

△ *Funnels.* The leader creates funnel shapes by laying ski poles on the hill. The widest part of the funnel is uphill, and a narrow opening is at the downhill end so that skiers must switch from a wedge to a straight-running position to squeeze through.

△ *Tree Crash Test.* The leader places a "tree" (a hat or other object) at midhill. Skiers head toward the tree and must stop in a wedge before it. If skiers can't stop they must sit down under control!

△ *Pie Trains.* Skiers ski behind partners in wedge positions, holding on to the front partner loosely. Skiers must be ready to separate if derailed!

△ *Red Light, Green Light.* The group spreads out across the top of a hill; the person who is the "traffic light" stands at the bottom. The traffic light faces away from the group and says "green light" for the skiers to begin snowplowing downhill. On "red light," all skiers must stop. The traffic light turns around to look at the group. Skiers who are still moving go back to the top. Skiers who have fallen but are stationary do not. The first skier to reach the finish line becomes the traffic light.

Common Problems and Corrections

Problem	Description	Correction
Knock Knees	Skiers create extreme edging with their skis.	Skiers keep their knees apart as if a basketball were between them.
Crossed Tips	Skiers stand unequally on their skis or overedge them.	Skiers need to stand equally on flattened skis and move them farther apart into a wider wedge.

Problem	Description	Correction
Hinging	This bent-over position inhibits good balance.	Skiers practice Touch the Sky to become upright and then practice Chair Sitting to keep a good flexed position.
Railing	One ski digs in sharply and tracks like a train on a rail. Too much weight is over the railed ski.	Skiers use the Snowplow Train on flat land to flatten the skis and make both legs work equally. They also repeat the Touch the Sky drill.
Inability to Stop	Skiers stand too upright, and their wedges are too narrow to brake against the snow.	Skiers flex their ankles and knees to "grow shorter," and they spread the skis wider. This should improve the edging. They can also try walking pigeon-toed down a gentle incline with their skis edged.

Wedge Turns (Snowplow Turns)

Once skiers are comfortable with controlling the basic position, they can try wedge turns. Introducing the turn from a narrower, gliding wedge works well because skiers have a comfortably high stance and begin from flatter skis. Only slight, shallow directional changes are necessary to effect a turn.

Skiers guide their skis through the turn by rotating their feet and legs in the direction of the turn. Leaders won't need to explain basic skills to children, who can sometimes turn almost magically by just looking in the direction they want to go! Just one gentle turn on a diagonal across the fall line is a good beginning.

As wedge turns become more pronounced, skiers add more steering, edging, skidding, and weight transfer naturally. They keep their hips centered and drop into a wider wedge to control their speed. They may also change the shape of their turns to affect their speed (Figure 4.21).

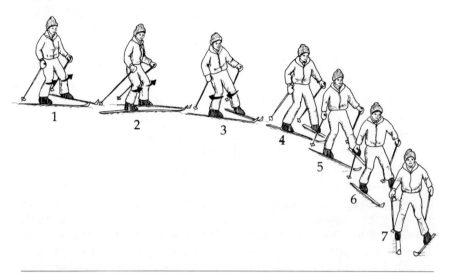

Figure 4.21. Wedge turns.

A complete description of the turn's components is too involved for young children. Leaders can set the right stage for practice with games and activities on a variety of types of terrain. The different bumps and dips of hills will teach children what to do.

Skills: sliding, steering, skidding, edging, moving from ski to ski

Basic Exercises

○ *Big Toe Theory.* Skiers place a ski pole between their ski tips, then press one ski tip sideways against the pole to feel how the big toe presses against the boot. They slide downhill in a wedge and press their big toes again. They point both big toes toward their destination and achieve magic turns!

○ *Knees Please.* Skiers repeat the Big Toe Theory to discover how their knees help to steer the skis. They watch the greater turning power of the skis when the knees follow the big toes.

○ *Pieces of the Pie.* The leader gives different names to narrow and wide slices of pie and calls out the names as skiers form the appropriate wedges. The leader should make the wide slices a favorite pie!

O   *Alphabet Turns.*   Skiers press their outside skis against the snow and watch the C-shaped path that the skis carve through the turn. They press harder and softer to change the C shape.

O   *Tractors.*   Skiers hold their arms straight out in front, pushing forward with one hand and pulling back with the other like levers on a tractor. They change the levers to turn the other way.

O   *Go Carts.*   Skiers hold a Frisbee in front as a steering wheel and steer around corners.

O   *Pole Points.*   Skiers hold a ski pole against the thigh of their outside leg. They point the pole in the direction of the turn.

O   *Headlights.*   Skiers hold both poles at their midpoint and place them against the outsides of and parallel to the thighs. The baskets become the headlights and should rest next to the knees. Skiers point the headlights to the route.

O   *Wedge Rebounds.*   Skiers step out into a wedge and bring their other skis parallel. They step back in the other direction and bring their skis parallel again. Skiers start on a gentle hill, stepping over the fall line. They perform the move in a bouncing, dancing fashion and rebound quickly from ski to ski. When the parallel stance is comfortable, they try steeper terrain. This is a good transition activity for older children and adolescents.

Activities

△   *Tandem Turning Plows.*   On flat terrain, one skier is the plow and the other skier (with or without skis) is the engine. The engine pushes the plow while it veers to one side and then the other. This is great for making the plow's legs do the work! Skiers can try a slalom course or plow a winding mountain road!

△   *Compass Bearings.*   The leader identifies the points on a compass (south is the bottom of a hill). Skiers are compasses and their skis are the compass needle. They head south, then turn their skis east or west. They can use a landmark like "the biggest tree in the east" and point their skis directly toward it.

△   *Taller, Smaller.*   Skiers stand tall and sink into a turn by bending at their knees and ankles (pressing their shins against their boots). They stand tall again to flatten the skis, then bring them together, point them down the hill, and sink the other way.

△   *Point A to B.*   The leader establishes a start and finish. Skiers travel from the start to the finish, making as many turns as possible. Skiers try to improve their first record by doing more turns.

△ *Slalom Courses.* A straight-line course encourages narrower wedges and quicker turns with the legs and feet. An offset course requires wider wedges and more pronounced turns. Skiers practice on different courses, keeping their upper bodies pointed toward the upcoming pole.

Common Problems and Corrections

Problem	Description	Correction
See Common Problems and Corrections for wedges.		
Overactive Upper Body	Skiers swing their shoulders aggressively through the turn or dip them to put pressure on the skis.	Skiers use slalom courses, with which the skiers' torsos should face the next pole.

Christies

A christy is a skidded turn in which both skis are skidding on corresponding edges at some point in the turn. Christies can begin with a wedge and finish with the skis parallel, where the skis skid on the same edges. To accomplish the move, skiers must perform an edge change. They must transfer weight to the outside ski to move the inside ski into position (Figure 4.22). Children initially end in a wide stance when their skis are parallel, because the balanced position gives them the security to handle speed.

Getting children out of a wedge can be difficult, and they may be in middle childhood before they can accomplish a christy. The turns are easier if the skiers use medium to long radius (sweeping) arcs along the fall line on a nonthreatening slope. The leader should encourage skiers to skid first at the end of the turn and then throughout more and more of the christy.

Children develop the ability to use many skills in an overlapping fashion. Skidding is the focus of many of the practice activities, but other skills are important. Skiers need to develop two-legged steering to shape a turn.

Children will sideslip their skis through the christy, because this is fun and it feels good! Sideslipping involves a skidding of the skis to the side and forward down the hill. But extensive skidding develops

Figure 4.22.   Christies.

sloppy turns. Children will readily accept the goal of carved turns to handle greater speed!

Skills: sliding, skidding, steering, moving from ski to ski, edging, poling

Basic Exercises

O   *Snow Trains.*   Skiers traverse on the rails (the path) and turn at the station (markers) with a gliding wedge. Skiers must be back on the rails between each turn.

O   *Eating Pizza.*   Skiers cut a piece of pizza at the corner (make a wedge) and gobble it up (move their skis parallel).

O   *Outer Space.*   Skiers use a long traverse across the fall line and a gliding wedge around a planet (a marker). The skiers are often comfortable enough to spontaneously skid and match the skis in a christy.

Using a wide slalom course of planets, skiers can steer their space-ships with both skis.

O *Hot Air Balloons*. Skiers traverse across the hill and lift off like hot air balloons at the corner. This encourages a lifting of the body that helps skiers skid and match their skis.

O *Sideslipping*. Skiers stand across the fall line with the skis parallel and slide sideways with tiny steps. They slide longer and longer before edging to stop.

O *Tip Slides*. Skiers turn their ski tips downhill, let the skis sideslip, and then let the skis bite the snow to stop.

O *One-Ski Sideslipping*. Skiers use only one ski and try sideslipping with just the downhill leg, then the uphill leg. Which is harder? They face the other way and try it again.

O *Mirror Images*. Skiers make their skis match completely when edging, sideslipping, and stopping. Skiers place equal pressure on each ski.

O *Tail Slides*. Skiers let their ski tails point downhill first to begin the sideslipping.

O *One-Legged Christy Garlands*. Skiers remove one ski. Making the outside leg the "skiing leg," they keep doing christies in one direction. The path of the turns will be like garlands on a Christmas tree. Then skiers change the skiing leg to the one on the inside of the turn. The legs on the inside and outside of the turn learn their jobs this way.

O *Hockey Stops*. Skiers stop as abruptly as possible, creating a spray of snow. This appealing challenge is highly visual, and children love to spray higher plumes of snow.

O *Plane Take-Offs*. Once skiers have begun the turn from a wedge, they lift their arms and bodies like planes taking off. This rising of the body helps skiers stand on the outside skis and move the inside skis into a parallel position for the runway landing.

Activities

△ *Sideslip Flips*. Skiers sideslip and turn 180 degrees. They count the number of times they turn 180 degrees in a given distance.

△ *Sideslip Lanes*. The leader marks wide travel lanes (a few feet longer than ski length) down the hill with poles or rope. Skiers side-slip and turn 180 degrees within this path. This forces quicker slide-slipping! Skiers practice first, then count the number of 180-degree turns. They can try to increase the number of turns along the course.

△ *Sideslip Command Posts*. Using the same travel lanes, the leader establishes command posts (markers) at specific spots where skiers must turn 180 degrees. As they improve, the leader puts the command posts closer together for a greater challenge or develops staggered locations (close and far apart) to see if skiers can handle irregular turning.

△ *Outrigger Turns.* Skiers turn on their inner skis and let their outside legs extend far to the outside as a counterbalance.

△ *Funnels.* Skiers begin with long, gradual christy turns and make them shorter and quicker. The turns "funnel" to a finish, where extremely quick turns occur along the fall line (Figure 4.23).

Figure 4.23. Funnels require progressively tighter turns.

△ *Snow Snake Patterns.*   Skiers look at the tracks created by the skis and try to narrow the angle of the skis. They blur the snake pattern on the inside of the turn by letting the skis float across the snow. Skiers move toward parallel snow snakes and away from angled skis.

Common Problems and Corrections

Problem	Description	Correction
Catching the Inside Ski	Skiers have too much weight and edging on the inside ski.	Skiers lift their bodies with Plane Take-Offs to let their skis move into a parallel stance. They also can try One-Legged Christies.
Weak Skidding	Skiers often have stiff legs	Skiers use sideslip-ping exercises with flexed legs. They can turn like a pogo stick. Skiers practice Plane Take-Offs at the end of the turn, then earlier in the turn as they improve.
Timing	The pole plants are irregular.	The leader uses a cadence to coor-dinate skiers' actions: plant-and-turn.
Excessive Skidding	The skis slide side-ways when more edging is needed to control the turn.	Skiers practice side-slipping activities to develop better control.

Parallel Turn

This turn keeps the skis in a parallel or equidistant stance from begin-ning to end. A parallel turn also begins to involve less skidding and more edging; it's a matter of degree on the skidding-carving continuum. Experienced skiers use a mix of skidded and carved turns. The more a turn is carved and the less it is skidded, the closer it is to a pure parallel turn (Figure 4.24).

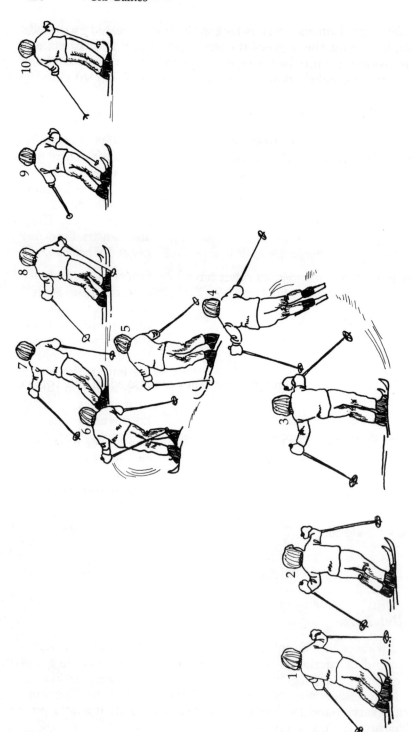

Figure 4.24. Parallel turn.

Initiating the turn with no wedging or stemming is the key to parallel skiing for young skiers. Leaders can set the stage with practice of christies, where the objective is matching the skis earlier and earlier in the turn. Being able to steer both skis independently through the turn is a good goal.

Again, children will adopt a sturdy, wide stance for increased stability. The wider stance offers good balance at the outset, with no need to glue the ankles together in the magazine image of the perfect parallel turn. As children develop "independent traction" in each leg to handle the differences in terrain, they begin to modify the wide stance to a narrower one.

When parallel turns are helped by more flexible up-and-down movements, the linked turns look smooth and rhythmic. Children often learn the timing of the poling by imitating the instructor. Children are capable of dynamic parallel technique that is a joy to watch.

Skills: sliding, gliding on one leg, moving from ski to ski, steering, edging, poling

Basic Exercises

O   *Boot Turns.*   Skiers take off their skis and practice swiveling their feet in place. (Skiers can use poles for balance.) Then they add motion with their knees for stronger pivoting. They can also add a little bounce to the swiveling. Then they try the sequence in place again with skis.

O   *Bunny Hops.*   Keeping the skis parallel, skiers rise up to hop from side to side. They stamp two parallel lines in the snow; keeping their legs springy.

O   *Tip Hops.*   Skiers keep their ski tips on the snow and lift their heels from side to side. They keep their knees limber, their skis parallel, and spring from side to side. They can move their skis farther apart by springing more powerfully.

O   *Walk on the Wild Side.*   Skiers walk and slide down the hill in a path like garlands on a Christmas tree (skiers keep turning in the same direction). They step strongly to the outside ski when creating each garland and keep turning uphill slightly. Then they create garlands by steering both legs uphill.

O   *Stork Turns.*   Skiers head down a moderate hill in a straight run. They press down on one of their skis and lift the other slightly. Then they turn both skis in the same direction.

O   *Running Bunnies.*   Skiers hop from side to side on a gradual downhill. They let their skis edge to prevent too much skidding.

O   *King of the Mountain.*   Skiers stand on top of a mogul and swivel their skis to feel how easy it can be. They try it in a dip! Ugh!

O   *Bounce Turns.*   Skiers bounce upward to turn like a bouncing ball making their legs very springy. Then they dampen the effect to a slight rising.

O   *Wedge Rebounds.*   Skiers step into a wedge with one of their skis and bring the other ski parallel. They repeat in the other direction. They step quickly across the fall line and rebound in a bouncy fashion—the quicker the better.

O   *Rocket Turns.*   Skiers crouch down on the launch pad as the corner approaches and lift off like a rocket. Both legs are boosters to steer through the turns.

O   *Glove Turns.*   Skiers place a glove or hat between their thighs before trying to turn. This encourages a tight stance!

O   *Magic Poles.*   Skiers touch their poles softly to the snow while turning.

O   *Electric Poles.*   Skiers touch their poles sharply to the snow while turning. Electrifying!

Activities

△   *Round the Mountain.*   Skiers traverse toward the mountain (a bump or mogul), plant the downhill pole as they climb the mountain, steer around the summit, and descend the other side. Then they climb bigger mountains!

△   *Synchronized Skiing.*   Partners ski side by side and synchronize their moves, changing from wider to narrower turns every four times (Figure 4.25).

Figure 4.25.   Synchronized Skiing.

△ *Follow the Leader.*   Skiers are in partners. The lead skier calls out changes in turns (short, medium, or long), and the follower matches the turns. The speed of descent never changes! Skiers switch roles.

△ *Satellite Turns.*   Skiers pretend to carry a satellite dish at their abdomens with their hands (and poles) framing the dish; skiers turn to ESPN on one side and HBO on the other.

△ *Symmetrical Poling.*   Skiers see how symmetrical poling increases their balance while skiing. They hold their inside poling hands lower to plant the pole and their outside hands higher for balance. These actions are subtle changes in the height of the hands from the snow. A nice rhythmic change in hand position occurs.

△ *Pickpocket.*   On the uphill side, skiers rotate their bodies so their uphill hands can "pick" their back pockets. This exaggerated exercise makes skiers feel the effects of early counter-rotation of the body. It might feel strange at first, but it makes the turn a solid one.

△ *C Shapes.*   Skiers feel a pinch at the waist when the body makes a crimped C-shape into the hill. They feel how the C changes from side to side in linked turns.

△ *Pinball.*   Skiers ski down a narrow corridor with many sharp turns. They imagine they are pinballs bounding off the walls. Then they soften the rebound so they are barely touching the wall.

△ *Walk on the Fall Line.*   Skiers turn along the fall line by stepping strongly onto each outside ski. They should begin on a gentler hill, or the speed is exciting!

△ *Paraskates.*   Skiers skate along the snow in a garland, skate onto the uphill ski, and use a parallel turn to round the corner. They skate along a traverse and skate onto the new uphill ski to turn the next corner.

Common Problems and Corrections

Problem	Description	Correction
See Common Problems and Corrections for christies.		
Speed Control	Insufficient edging is often the cause.	Skiers finish each turn by digging in the edges more sharply; they step uphill to initiate the turn and transfer weight dynamically.

Problem	Description	Correction
Sitting Back	The skier's weight rests on his or her heels.	Skiers flex their ankles and knees, which helps them to steer well. They act like "midget" skiers to begin the turns and lean their torsos down the hill in anticipation of the next turn.
Changing Snow Conditions	Skiers may stall in deeper or wetter snow.	Skiers strive for stronger steering with both legs and greater lift or rise with the entire body. They should use more muscle in general to bring the skis around!

Telemark Turn

The telemark is skiing's oldest turn, and cave drawings attest to its venerable status. Spindly drawings show skiers in the distinctive "curtsy" that identifies the telemark. The turn is experiencing a rebirth among Nordic skiers, whose free heels allow them to sink into the telemark position.

Practicing the basic telemark position is essential. A skier slides one ski forward and sinks until the heel lifts off the other ski. The body is straight with the shoulder and hip directly above the knee of the trailing leg. Weight is equally distributed between the skis. The instructor must not rush the practice of the basic position, because poor turns usually stem from a problem with body position (Figure 4.26).

Once skiers assume the telemark position, they steer both skis in the new direction. Both skis extend into a long, stable platform and function almost as one ski. The skiers skid and edge the skis to turn them.

Because the telemark lowers a skier's body, it is a very secure turn. Its stability is apparent in its use by ski jumpers as a landing technique. Children love Olympic themes, and the idea of a ski jumper landing in a telemark position is incentive for them to learn it. They search for bumps to pop off and land in the telemark position.

Figure 4.26.   Telemark position.

Four- and five-year-olds instinctively use the position to increase their balance. Because their strength is limited, they often can't get back up, though! I've seen 6-year-olds perform nicely linked telemarks after good coaching by their telemarking parents.

Skills: sliding, steering, skidding, edging, poling

Basic Exercises

O   *Change-Ups.*   Skiers sink into a telemark position in place, then rise to an upright stance and sink on the other side. They should change positions smoothly.

O   *Pop-Ups.*   Skiers pop between telemark positions by springing off their skis.

O   *Telemark Striding.*   Skiers stride across the snow and sink into a telemark every third stride. They repeat this exercise on a gentle hill (without turning).

O   *Partner Pulls.*   Two skiers stand across the hill, one below the other and holding onto poles stretched between them. The uphill skier sinks into the telemark position (downhill ski leads). The downhill skier pulls gradually on the poles until the uphill skier is aggressively leaning down the hill. The upper body is set up for linked turns.

O   *Telly Traverses.*   Skiers traverse the hill and sink into a telemark (downhill ski leads). Their shoulders should face downhill. On a long hill, skiers stand up and sink into the telemark position repeatedly. They should try for rhythmic motions!

O   *Half-Wedge Tellies.*   From a straight run, skiers use a half-wedge to begin the turn and sink into the telemark position when coming through the fall line.

O   *Skating Tellies.*   Skiers traverse a hill by skating, skate onto the uphill ski, and sink into a telemark turn to round the corner.

O   *Squirt Turns.*   Skiers shift their weight toward their heels during the turn and squirt forward.

O   *Tight Dress Turns.*   Skiers sink into the turns like they're wearing tight dresses and try to touch the ground. They should keep their legs close together!

O   *Cricket Turns.*   Skiers keep their thighs so close that they can rub their legs past each other like a cricket. This is a test for a good, tight stance.

O   *Leg Lifts.*   Skiers lift their outside legs to step forward into the turn. This move momentarily weights the inside skis completely and prevents them from skidding around weightless.

O   *Leg Pumps.*   Skiers traverse a hill and "pump" their uphill skis several times while in the telemark position. This is a great rhythmic, floating feeling. Then they sink into a telemark turn by sliding their uphill skis forward and steering them around the corner.

O   *Leg Retractions.*   Rather than sliding a ski forward, skiers retract one of their legs and sink into the turn.

O   *Ski Pointers.*   Skiers point one of their hands at the tips and the other at the tails of their skis (when skiers' torsos are facing downhill during the turn). Pointing exaggerates the upper body position, but it gets skiers to separate their torsos from their legs.

O   *The Bomber.*   Skiers ski down the fall line and do many quick turns by steering briefly but sharply with the leading foot.

Activities

△   *Funnels.*   Skiers use long, gradual telemark turns and then shorten them progressively until short, quick turns finish the funnel. Is the funnel regular in shape?

△   *Giant Slalom.*   The leader sets a course with offset poles for wide, graceful turns.

△ *Group Telemarks.* Skiers try turning with a partner or small and large groups. The greater the number, the more likely a pigpile (Figure 4.27)!

Figure 4.27. Tandem Telemarks.

△ *Monomarks.* Skiers use one telemark position and turn in both directions by changing the edges of the skis.

△ *Step Telemarks.* Skiers step into a wedge and sink into a telemark. The outside ski leads into the turn. Then the skiers rise, step into a wedge again, and sink into a telemark with the new outside leg leading into the turn. This two-step telemark makes skiers cross the fall line each time, while the skis brake strongly. This is a great way to step down a steep hill.

△ *Step Telemark Race.* The leader establishes a course between two points and counts the number of step telemarks between the points. The skier who does the most turns on the course wins.

△ *Step Telemark Dance.* Skiers ski in partners. The lead skier sets a slow pace by creeping down the hill in step telemarks. The follower tries to move as slowly and with equal control.

△ *Jump Turns.* Skiers ski straight down a moderate hill, leap between telemarks, and jump over an imaginary line. In new snow, the leader marks a line for skiers to leap over.

Common Problems and Corrections

Problem	Description	Correction
Poor Telemark Position	The rear leg trails with little weight on the ski. Or skiers crouch in an almost-parallel stance.	Skiers return to the basic exercises to memorize the proper position (Figure 4.28).

Figure 4.28. Poor telemark positions.

Problem	Description	Correction
Crossing Tails	Skis are not weighted equally, and the inside ski floats around to cross the other.	Skiers use the Leg Lift exercise. They review the basic telemark position and move into it by standing first on the tentative leg.
Skidding Out	Skiers' shoulders swing through the turn and overpivot the skis.	Skiers use Partner Pulls and Ski Pointers to point their torsos down the hill.
Stemming	Skis stay apart and don't slide together into a "monoski."	Skiers need stronger steering by the inside foot. Big Toe, Knees Please, and Hip Tricks exercises for snowplow turns will help develop independent steering by both legs.
Railing	Skis are overedged in the turn.	Skiers use the Touch the Sky exercise to lift the body and flatten the skis.

Skate Turn

The skate turn is a way to change directions without losing speed. In fact, a skate turn helps a skier to accelerate around a corner, and children with good balance will discover this move quickly.

From a traverse, the skier steps off the outside ski and glides onto the inside ski. During the turn, the outside ski is edged strongly to provide a strong push onto the gliding ski. The V-shaped position of the skis allows for the change of direction. The skier can end in a parallel stance or keep skating across the hill (Figure 4.29).

With the emergence of skating in Nordic skiing, children are proving to be versatile skaters. They feel that it's not that different from ice or roller skating, and this familiarity with the basic moves enables them

Figure 4.29. Skate turn.

to develop comfort quickly. They begin to look as aggressive as their Alpine counterparts.

The speed of a skate turn distinguishes it from a step turn—"the turn of a thousand steps"—with which skiers ride the momentum and use many little steps to walk around the corner. Skate turns feel like "rockets" as skiers blast around the corner. Hard double poling can also increase the speed!

Skills: sliding, gliding on one ski, moving from ski to ski, edging, pushing off, poling

Basic Exercises

O   Skiers use the basic (no pole) skating exercises.

O   *Star Turns.*   Skiers plant a ski pole at the tails of their skis. They step around the pole by opening the tips of their skis and keeping the tails near the pole. They take small steps at first, then bigger ones.

Activities

△   *Figure Eights.*   Skiers play follow the leader along an oval, then weave a figure eight pattern. Skiers use skate turns at each end and have to use strategies to negotiate the intersection without bumping into another skier. Using one ski at the beginning increases traffic control.

△   *Flatland Slalom.*   This is a great way to encourage skate turns! A challenging goal is negotiating the course with only one skate turn around each pole. The leader can move the poles farther apart to present a real challenge.

△   *Rocket Turns.*   The leader plants one pole on a corner, and skiers must perform a skate turn at the marker then finish by gliding as far as possible on two skis. The object is pushing hard off the outside ski to get good glide (Figure 4.30).

Figure 4.30.   Rocket Turns.

△ *Double Rocket Turns.* The leader establishes two side-by-side courses, each with a marker, and a line of skiers for each course. The two skiers at the head of the lines are paired. They ski down and skate turn at the markers at the same time. (They have to turn away from each other to avoid a collision.) Each pair continues the synchronized skiing back to the end of the line. Pairs keep skiing to develop a revolving circle of skiers. Skiers get lots of good, active practice with this one.

△ *Razor's Edge.* Skiers must travel along a trail junction with a sharp corner that requires more than one skate turn.

△ *Skate Garlands.* Skiers skate across a hill, stepping uphill strongly. They skate around a corner and continue the traverse. The garland patterns encourage strong pushing to move slightly uphill.

Common Problems and Corrections

Problem	Description	Correction
Poor Pushing Off	Skiers need to improve their ability to balance on one ski. Rapid weight shifts inhibit their ability to spring off the outside ski.	Skiers remember the Toe-Knee-Nose rule and take smaller steps.
Poor Balance	Falling to the inside of the turn is often a problem. It is usually a function of speed.	Skiers move to milder terrain to practice moving smoothly from ski to ski. Skiers take smaller, quicker steps. Bigger ones will come when one-legged balance improves.

5 *Games*

Playing games with skiing is an exciting process that never ends. Any activity can be modified endlessly, and children are experts at proposing a new twist. Many of the exciting elements in the activities in this book were proposed by kids who wanted to try one more challenge. Their excitement about the sport leaves them begging for more, and ready to suggest how to do it!

You don't have to be a ski instructor to develop good games. Every person is a valuable resource of games and activities. Formal and informal play is a part of our lives, and these experiences offer many creative ideas that we can bring to the ski playground.

I watched the growing awareness of a talented parent in an instructor training session and knew this man would be his neighborhood's best catalyst for future skiers. Not a particularly talented skier, he joined the session to improve his skiing skills and to find out how he could teach his children and their friends.

As we demonstrated various lighthearted exercises to develop specific skills, the parent tentatively suggested an alternative. With every skill, he thought of additional games. We played them all. His creative mind was a gold mine of possibilities, and by the day's end, our notes were filled with his proposals.

Use these games as a basis for endless variations. Be flexible, and change the rules to suit various ages. Establish the rules that your group needs for safe, enjoyable play. Beneath the laughter, game playing is an organized approach that requires much structure and often requires more work on the instructor's part. The rewards are great, however, because the children are invested in the process and they progress farther than they might in a less active program.

Safe and Enjoyable Play

Snow is a great playground when a few good guidelines are used to shape the nature of skiers' activities. Fast-paced action on a slippery surface with lots of players requires special considerations to promote safety and enjoyment. Safety can be promoted wisely and well by leaders who understand how to encourage good playing. Children need to understand that safety is their responsibility when skiing.

Play helps to increase children's awareness and to steer them away from aggressive, risky performances. By playing more cooperatively in partnerships or as a total group, children learn to play more safely and with good spirit. They possess a greater repertoire of intriguing tasks and games that they can share with others. While children may still be drawn to high-speed action and high-flying jumps, they won't necessarily rely on those activities if there are other activities from which to choose. This is an important issue in young skiers' continued learning and safety.

During a weekend ski lesson, my adult class arrived at one of the usual practice areas to try some turning exercises, and we found four kids playing on some mild bumps and dips in the terrain. One of the boys yelled my name, and I realized that he had been in one of my public school programs the preceding week.

"Watch this," he said. He led his friends through a series of synchronized dance moves that I had encouraged in the class. None of the friends had been in the class, but they had obviously been practicing. They had also experimented with some new moves that we hadn't tried in the lesson. My student had turned into a teacher.

"We're up to eight things until we're not together anymore," he said proudly.

I was thrilled to see these kids respond to such a challenge. In the class, I had wanted to see smooth transitions between different types of turns regardless of the terrain. The task, to ski in unison, was easier to meet with flowing moves rather than jarring ones, and these boys had discovered that secret.

Tricky of me? Absolutely! But these challenges encourage children to keep playing with the sport, and they appeal to them in a healthy way. Forget a Tail-End Charlie bringing up the rear or an I-dare-you-to-try-this leader of the pack. The kids are drawn to other challenging alternatives that are fun.

Basic Organization

Any poorly executed approach risks failure, and game playing is no exception. The increased activity can be difficult to control, and establishing ground rules for safe play is a necessity. An instructor must be ready to blow the whistle or call "time out" to stop the action.

Organizing safe, enjoyable games is a stiff challenge but an exhilarating one. Let's look at some basic guidelines for developing safe and enjoyable play.

The Objective. Behind every game is a hidden agenda for the children. Each game incorporates different variables, and the leader matches the activities to the needs of each child.

The activities differ in the fundamental skills and techniques that they emphasize. The leader must make conscious decisions to choose the most appropriate play. For instance, if skiers can't stop well on a hill, they should return to the flats with an activity that emphasizes snowplows.

Good activities are simple and avoid confusion. They have a few, clear objectives that can be met and they vary in intensity and duration.

Duration. The instructor must avoid running a good game into the ground. Stop it when skiers still want more!

Intensity. Intense activities may be exhausting, so the instructor must call time-outs to rest or just to breathe!

Total Participation. Everyone plays, and no one stands on the sidelines! Games that eliminate players often stop the practice of those who need it the most. Instructors must choose activities that encourage continuous play to increase practice. Such activities also keep all players warm!

Role of Leader. The leader or teacher should play with the players! Leaders must be careful of being an observer or director, who can subtly affect the quality of the activity.

However, a referee is needed in some activities to control boisterous action. In such cases, the leader should keep moving and coach from the sidelines.

Fair Teams. Leaders should use creative ways to choose partnerships or teams, such as grouping people with birthdays in months beginning with J or telling skiers to "find someone whose legs are the same length as yours." Leaders should avoid the socially disastrous effects of having captains choose teams (what if nobody picks me?) or letting children group themselves (do they really want me to be part of this group?).

Here are more suggestions. Each skier finds a partner who is wearing the same color as he or she. Skiers pick a number from one to five and hold up that number of fingers. Everyone showing an even number of fingers is on one team; those holding up an odd number go to the other team. Each skier picks a partner who is his or her height. Or, skiers with blue parkas are on one team, and those with purple parkas are on the other team.

Cooperation or Competition?   Instructors should choose more activities that encourage children to play with rather than against others. Activities should emphasize enjoyment through participation rather than keeping score. Competition against oneself can be valuable, and "personal best" activities encourage a child to beat his or her individual record.

Competition is not always bad, and within a group it can encourage a cooperative team to try harder. But the activities that declare winners should be extremely limited in number. Children can adopt a "winning" mentality that interferes with their learning of new activities and their appreciation for everyone's right to learn at their own speed.

Terrain.   The leader should clearly establish the playing field and choose terrain that helps skiers meet the objective of an activity. The playground should match skiers' abilities and the required action. The terrain should work in the skier's favor.

Speed is a big factor in some games, which are best played on flat terrain. Wide open slopes lend themselves to fewer collisions and a better view of the action than narrower trails. But a large group can be hard to organize in wide open spaces, as skiers will disperse in all directions! Trails make it easier to direct a group as long as everyone knows the next destination and they stop at the intersections!

The same terrain can affect skiers differently. Bumps and dips can intimidate beginners, but they can actually help more experienced skiers to turn.

Collisions.   Instructors should avoid activities that lend themselves to collisions and pigpiles. Tasks in which children converge on a central point can be dangerous, because tangled bodies and equipment can lead to injuries.

Instructors should choose activities in which players must have clear, open spaces around them to play well. Throwing balls and keeping them in the air is a safer task than a game that requires kicking a ball with skis.

"Soft" props or items that will give way upon impact also enhance safety. Using people as obstacles or destinations is questionable, as skiers may not be able to avoid them.

Players should tag each other by throwing a hat or mitten rather than by skiing close and touching each other. The throwing helps skiers to keep their distance.

Poles. Instructors should eliminate poles in high-action activities where children can fall on the poles or poke them at others. Pole tips can become inadvertent weapons in games with a lot of dodging and darting.

Skiers can often learn to move more efficiently without poles, and eliminating them can be a blessing to more timid skiers, who often loosen up once they have eliminated their white-knuckled grip on the poles.

Minimal Rules. Instructors should establish a few simple rules and see that skiers adhere to them. Wordy explanations are boring and often forgotten, and a long list of "don'ts" is confusing. Instructors should choose several important rules that children can remember, such as the following.

- Don't ski over another person's skis.
- Be able to ski around people who have fallen.
- Do not charge or push other skiers.
- Let go of your partner if you are going to fall.

Traffic Patterns. Skiers must observe the rules of the road! Good routes and clear boundaries for activities help to reduce confusion. Instructors can designate "up" and "down" travel lanes on hills and choose play areas and routes away from trail sides and trees. If circular routes are used, the instructor should establish a protocol for overtaking another skier.

Controlled Falling. Effective falling is a defensive tactic in a game—it enhances everyone's safety. Children should fall to the sides of their skis and stand up quickly. Skis in the air can be a hazard to others, especially at face level. If necessary, the instructor should call a time-out if too many skiers fall in the middle of the action.

Number of Players. The number of participants can affect the type of play. Some activities are more exciting with a large group, while others are safer with fewer people. The best games can fail with the wrong group. The instructor must be ready to change the game plan quickly.

Boot Games

Many cooperative games on land are perfect for use in an orientation to the ski playground. Boot games eliminate any problems with cumbersome skis and keep the youngest children active on snow. They help make the snowy playground a desirable place.

A 2-year-old who is frustrated with his or her skis can still develop important skills with these activities. They are a wonderful way to begin a program to get children oriented to the snow, and they also work well at the conclusion when children are tired.

The boot games allow more freedom of movement, and they make it easier for a child to fall down and get up. They help Alpine skiers get used to the heavy boots and help develop other important skills like independent leg action and good balance.

Old favorites include Duck, Duck, Goose; Red Light, Green Light; Simon Says; and the Hokeypokey, among others. These games lend themselves to variations once children are wearing their skis. Introducing the games as boot games and returning to them after the children are on skis helps even the littlest skiers see their own progress.

The activities are suitable for children from 2 to 6 years. Children who are slightly older but who have difficulty moving easily may welcome them, too.

Recommended terrain is flat land.

☆ HUGS

The instructor establishes a small play area where the children can walk around without bumping into each other. The children listen as the leader sings a song, and when the music stops they must hug another person. As the leader begins to sing again, they walk around holding hands with their partner. When the song stops, each pair hugs another pair. Gradually, the entire group hugs each other when the song stops (Figure 5.1).

Figure 5.1. Hugs.

☆ *Safety Tip: Children may stumble while they're hugging others, so the instructor should be prepared to pick them up a lot. They may get tangled!*

☆ LOG ROLLS

Partners lie down on the snow with the bottoms of their boots touching. They roll over and try to keep their boots touching as they roll. In soft snow, teams can pave a path that winds or curves into a circle. This game results in lots of giggling and admiring of the final route!

☆ *Safety Tip: Children can veer wildly in this one. Each team must have plenty of room.*

☆ MOVING BRIDGES

In this game, 5- and 6-year-olds can move quickly. Everyone chooses a partner, and the pairs line up in follow-the-leader fashion. The partners at the head of the line create a bridge with their arms, which everyone ducks under. As soon as the second pair of skiers duck under the bridge, they create another bridge with their arms. Every pair builds a bridge when they finish coming through the tunnel of arms. A group can travel around a field, around trees, and up and down small hills with these moving bridges.

☆ *Safety Tip: This activity also works on skis, but the terrain has to be absolutely flat to avoid collisions.*

☆ DRAGON'S TAIL

Each child wears a bright streamer, ribbon, or handkerchief tucked into the back of his or her pants or tied loosely around the waist (so it comes undone when pulled). The leader establishes boundaries for a playing field and identifies a child to be "it." He or she runs around trying to grab a tail. Every tagged player freezes, and they try to grab other tails as players run past them. Eventually, only one child is left moving on the field—the next "it."

☆ *Safety Tip: Skiers can try this one on skis, too! But the streamer should be much longer so that it sweeps on the ground. Then children won't get their skis tangled up.*

☆ TRAINS

This game has lots of variations! Everyone chooses a partner, and one person holds onto the other's hips from behind. Each pair pretends to be a car on a train. The cars can follow an established track, hop off and get derailed, and move backward. Then the cars can link up and create one large train. The train can travel around the field, up and down hills, and around corners. (Children can try it with skis. The cars can hold onto each other's hands so they don't trip over their skis.)

☆ *Safety Tip: Some children trip and fall when the train begins to form, especially if the pace is too fast. They should go slowly!*

☆ RUNAWAY TRAINS

Teams of two or three children form cars by holding onto each other's hips. They move as a unit around an established area. One child is designated the caboose, and he or she has to chase the other cars and tag them for a link-up. Once a caboose tags a car, the caboose links onto the tail end of the group. The leader of that car becomes the new caboose.

☆ *Safety Tip: This game lends itself to wearing skis if the players hold hands so they don't stumble over the skis.*

☆ ALPHABET

This exercise involves the entire group as everyone tries to build a letter of the alphabet with his or her body. One player shouts out a letter, and then everyone scrambles to lie down in the right positions. Of course, this creates lots of confusion, and children have to move around to get in the right place. Squirming on stomaches and crawling into place is part of the fun. Large groups of 7-year-olds have spelled words!

☆ *Safety Tip: Children need to be careful of their hard boots and encouraged not to kick others.*

☆ BEACH BALL TUNNELS

Without skis, the players line up in follow-the-leader fashion and spread their legs to create a tunnel. The child at the head of the line pushes a ball between his or her legs to the next player and then runs to the end of the line. Meanwhile, the next player pushes the ball along and then peels off. Later, the children can play the same game wearing skis, lining their skis up tip to tail. The ball can bounce outside the tunnel, though, and it takes time to chase the ball while wearing skis. The instructor can divide a large group into smaller teams so everyone gets lots of action (Figure 5.2).

☆ *Safety Tip: Children should have enough space between them so they don't knock each other down when pushing the ball.*

Figure 5.2. Beach Ball Tunnels.

☆ PINBALL

Children stand in a large circle and hold hands. They kick a ball around the circle and keep it inside the circle by kicking it with their legs. Then the circle begins to revolve, and they have to keep the ball moving while they are moving. This game is great with lots of kids because there are fewer holes in the circle.

> ☆ *Safety Tip: This game works well with skis as long as players are cautioned against lifting their ski tips high or toward another person.*

☆ BARNYARD

The instructor establishes a playing area in an imaginary barnyard with fields, corrals, and a barn. Each team of three players chooses an animal that makes a good noise: roosters, cows, horses, cats, or dogs! A member of each team stands in each different area (field, corral, or barn). Everyone closes their eyes. On "go," each member tries to find the rest of the team, and they link up. The only way to find teammates is by making the team noise.

> ☆ *Safety Tip: Children should move slowly and get up quickly if they fall down. Otherwise, they can knock others down.*

Ski Games

Each section lists the target skills and techniques for the activity. Some games involve many techniques, and only the major emphasis is highlighted.

☆ ELBOW TAG

Skills: *all except poling*
Techniques: *skating, wedges*
Terrain: *flat with a square playing field with boundaries*
Age: *middle childhood, adolescence*

This is an active game that keeps everyone moving! Children play it while wearing only one ski; this helps them stop and turn with fewer collisions. Players can't be tagged when they have linked elbows with a partner and are facing in opposite directions. Another player can take advantage of this safety zone by linking arms with one of the skiers. (It's a great way to take a rest!) The skier at the opposite end of the threesome must let go and ski away. That skier is now free to be tagged. The person who is "it" tags a free person by throwing a hat or mitten at the player. "It" changes quickly in this game.

The game calls for lots of quick changes of direction and great inter-action among players. Children who have problems with stopping can play with one ski. The instructor can stop the game periodically to allow players to change skiing legs. Players who can brake well can play with both skis (Figure 5.3).

Figure 5.3. Elbow Tag.

☆ *Safety Tip: The instructor calls time-outs if players begin to fall near each other in their enthusiasm. Play resumes when everyone is separated (and upright)!*

☆ PIE TAG

Skills: all except poling
Techniques: wedges
Terrain: flat or gently hilly with a square playing field with boundaries
Age: preschool, middle childhood

Skiers choose their favorite pie. To avoid being tagged, they make a pie shape with their skis and shout out their favorite kind of pie. Pie positions can last only five seconds, so players must keep moving!

☆ SAMURAI WARRIOR

Skills: balancing on one ski, moving from ski to ski
Techniques: falling down and getting up!
Terrain: flat
Age: all

The samurai stands in the center of a big circle of ski warriors—about 10 feet away from them. (Each warrior has plenty of room to fall down without hitting another person.) The samurai bows to the warriors, who return the bow politely. Then the action begins. If the samurai swings his sword (ski pole) at the warriors' feet, they must leap into the air. If the sword swirls above their heads, they must duck. Warriors must watch out for quick changes in the sword's direction! Yells from the samurai intensify the action.

The samurai "wounds" the warriors when he or she points the sword directly at them. Warriors must fall down, get up, and bow to the samurai to re-enter the game. A great ending is "wounding" the whole army to make sure that everyone falls. It puts everyone on equal "footing." Despite the warlike sound of the game, it's a funny, low-key icebreaker to get skiers relaxed and limber (Figure 5.4).

☆ *Safety Tip: The skiers keep far away from the ski pole. The player in the middle holds the ski basket so the grip faces the skiers.*

☆ SIMON SAYS

Skills: all
Techniques: instructor chooses which ones need practice!
Terrain: flat or hilly
Age: preschool, middle childhood

Figure 5.4.   Samurai Warrior.

This is a snowy variation of a well-known favorite! Simon (the leader) begins the game by focusing on skills and asking skiers to perform various tasks, like "Simon says lift one leg, bend over, bend your knees, step sideways, take a giant step to the side, rock from ski to ski, run in place, point your ski this way. . . ."

On hills, the leader can ask for different types of turns as skiers slowly begin their descent. When "Simon Says" doesn't precede the request, skiers must stop immediately. Skiers who don't stop quickly must go back uphill to a spot behind the last person. The entire group can stay together as a moving unit.

☆   *Safety Tip: Each skier has a separate lane down the hill and aims for his or her own spot to cross the finish line.*

☆ RED LIGHT, GREEN LIGHT

Skills: *all*
Techniques: *the skiers choose their best!*
Terrain: *flat or hilly with a start line and a finish line*
Age: *preschool, middle childhood*

Here's another classic applied to snow! The object is to cross the finish line first, but stopping on the "red light" requires excellent use of braking wedges. The leader can give skiers a slight edge by facing away from the group, then calling "red light" before turning around to see who is still moving. As the skiers improve their quick stops, the leader turns around more quickly to look for moving players.

☆   *Safety Tip: Again, each skier has a separate lane to avoid converging at one spot at the bottom!*

☆ TOE THE LINE

Skills: *all*
Techniques: sidestepping and turns
Terrain: *flat*
Ages: *all*

Everyone stands side by side on a line. The leader calls out different tasks that the group members must perform as they reassemble and assume a new order on the line. It's a good way to get children moving on their skis and meeting each other at the beginning of a program. Players can line up alphabetically by first name, chronologically by birth date, or by height.

Players can also try lining up in clusters or groups along the line; they can line up by number of brothers or sisters, by color of their eyes, or by color of jackets or pants.

☆ SKI KEEP AWAY

Skills: *all except poling*
Techniques: skating
Terrain: *flat with a rectangular playing field with two goals*
Age: *middle childhood, adolescence*

Skiers are in two teams, each with a goal. Skiers must pass a ball to move it toward their goal (kicking the ball risks collisions). The best strategy is receiving the ball in an open space and passing to a teammate who is also in a clear position. Goals are scored by throwing the ball between the goal posts (Figure 5.5).

Figure 5.5. Ski Keep Away.

A ball dropped on the snow is dead, and possession goes to the other team at that spot. If a player touches opposing players or their skis, a personal foul is called. The touched player gets a free throw from the sidelines.

The successful team is the one that develops good strategies for passing the ball—not the team that skis the fastest. The leader uses a whistle to call the plays, because the action gets intense!

Four or five players work best on a small playing field. Older players and larger teams can handle a large field. Adolescents with good skiing skills can kick the ball rather than pass it, making the action more like Ski Soccer.

☆ *Safety Tip: If skiers have difficulty with stopping quickly, they can take off a ski. They'll have more control and just as much fun!*

☆ SHARKS AND MINNOWS

Skills: all except poling
Techniques: skating, skate turns
Terrain: flat with a rectangular playing field with safety zones at either end
Age: middle childhood, adolescence

One person is the shark in the middle of the field. The rest of the group, the minnows, stand in a safety zone. When the shark calls "shark attack," the minnows ski to the other safety zone to escape the shark. The shark tries to tag the minnows with a hat. When a minnow is tagged, he or she immediately becomes a shark and begins to tag other skiers. Soon a group of hungry sharks roam the field in search of a few lone minnows. This is a wonderfully active game!

☆ *Safety Tip: The playing field is wide enough that skiers have space to ski around players who fall. Players need lots of room to move.*

☆ SNAKE TAG

Skills: all except poling
Techniques: striding, wedge, and skate turns
Terrain: flat with a square playing field
Age: middle childhood, adolescence

At the outset, this wild game is best played with skiers on one ski. Otherwise, skiers end up tripping over the skis or flying away from the snake formation.

When "it" tags another skier, the two hold hands and begin to form a snake. The snake gets longer as "it" tags more skiers. The head and tail of the snake are "it," and they tag other players by throwing a hat or sponge.

Large groups can play Double or Triple Snake Tag by designating two or three "its" at the beginning. The game is wild if the tail of the snake gets whipped around a bit.

☆ *Safety Tip: Be careful the game doesn't turn into Whipchain!*

☆ HOKEYPOKEY

Skills: *all except poling*
Techniques: none
Terrain: *flat*
Age: *preschool*

Children stand in a circle and sing to the tune of the Hokeypokey: "You put one foot in, you put one foot out, you put one foot in, and you shake it all about. You do the Hokeypokey and you turn yourself around. That's what it's all about!" Players use their feet, arms, head, and whole self. They finish with everyone sliding into the center to circle up for one last rousing round.

☆ *Safety Tip: Children need adequate spacing. They'll keep try-*
         ing to move in closer. They need enough room to
         fall when they try to stand on one leg.

☆ TUG-OF-WAR

Skills: *all, especially edging*
Techniques: wedges
Terrain: *flat*
Age: *middle childhood, adolescence*

Skiers can play the tug-of-war facing each other in wedge positions or standing sideways with a wide stance. The object of the game remains the same—to pull the other team over a central line. Players use a length of rope that is long enough so that each player has enough space to fall without hitting another skier. Each version is an excellent test of edging skills.

☆ *Safety Tip: Skiers must be careful of sitting down hard or fall-*
         ing over abruptly. They can let go of the rope to
         ease a fall.

☆ SHIPWRECK

Skills: all except poling
Techniques: all
Terrain: flat with a rectangular playing field
Age: middle childhood, adolescence

This game involves lots of skiing and laughter when players have to perform the special commands. A captain directs the mates on this ship, who may use one or both skis depending upon their abilities. The leader establishes bow, stern, port, and starboard sides to the rectangular field. When the captain calls one of these directions, skiers race to cross that line.

The leader reviews the required action on the special commands: "Person overboard" means two skiers link elbows and face in opposite directions; "jellyfish" means everyone flops onto their back and waves arms and legs in the air; "man the torpedoes" means two skiers kneel down side by side and point their arms like cannons (Figure 5.6). When the captain makes a command, skiers must perform the tasks in the middle of the rectangle. They need to be careful of the "jellyfish" call and keep their skis low until all skiers are on their backs! If skiers play the game as an elimination game, the last skiers to follow the command become line judges. All ages love this one!

☆ *Safety Tip: Skiers must look for open spaces toward which to ski and avoid converging on one spot.*

☆ LEAP FROG

Skills: all
Techniques: instructor chooses the focus
Terrain: rolling or gently inclining
Age: middle childhood, adolescence

This activity requires a line of moving skiers and enables the group to travel around the ski area. The leader establishes a lead skier and a safe distance that skiers must remain apart to avoid collisions. The lead skier chooses a route and the techniques to move along it. The skiers follow along the trail or route until the lead skier stops abruptly causing skiers to veer in a new direction (chosen by the new lead skier at the head of the line). Everyone skis around the original lead skier and follows the new one. The old lead skier joins the end of the line. The veering works especially well with cross-country skiers, who are forced to change tracks. The Alpine lead can point in a new direction to move skiers away from him or her in a specific direction.

Figure 5.6. Shipwreck

☆ *Safety Tip: Skiers have different paces, but they must match the pace of the group for this game. They can't crowd the skier in front, and they need enough room to be able to ski around a person who falls.*

☆ BIATHLON

Skills: all
Techniques: instructor chooses the focus
Terrain: flat, rolling, or downhill
Age: all

The instructor establishes a course with several stations where skiers must perform certain tasks before they proceed (e.g., throw three tennis balls into a basket, roll three balls into the center of a hula hoop, throw three rings over a traffic cone, or roll three tennis balls into holes in the snow).

The instructor records individual times and encourages players to improve their own time. The instructor designates different techniques for succeeding runs to compare the difference in times or lets players choose their fastest technique.

For preschool children, the course should be tiny and the stations should require simple tasks. For instance, players try to place a ball in a large, deep crater dug in the snow.

☆ MINIATURE SNOW GOLF

Skills: all
Techniques: instructor chooses the focus
Terrain: rolling or downhill
Age   all

The instructor establishes another course with several stations where skiers must perform another set of tasks. The older the skiers are, the greater the distance between the stations. The instructor uses slalom poles, traffic cones, snow bridges, and tunnels to lay out the lanes and obstacles at each station. Each station can have several starting lines so more than one player can shoot for the hole. Skiers can roll tennis balls or use their poles to push a bigger ball along. The instructor can keep score if he or she has enough volunteers to help.

Again, preschool children need a very simple course. They like pushing a big ball along a snowy trench to a final hole or batting it under a bridge of snow. Rolling a ball from between their legs is good also.

☆ POLE JUNGLES

Skills: *all*
Techniques: *all, especially turns*
Terrain: *flat or gently inclining*
Age: *all*

The instructor sets up a maze of upright poles to match the group's abilities. The larger the group is, the more poles needed! For new skiers, poles should be farther apart! A random pattern requires skiers to make many changes to negotiate the poles. The instructor uses a variety of tasks: turn around four poles; enter next to a red pole and leave next to a blue one; do it backwards; turn twice on one leg; and follow another person. Skiers love these jungles. The instructor can ask them to set up their own course, and they'll put the poles closer together to make it harder (Figure 5.7)!

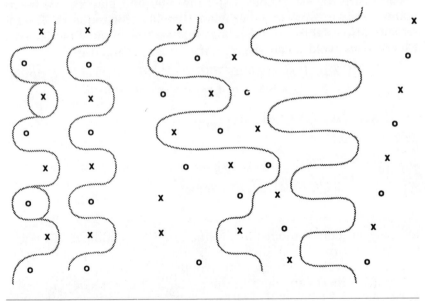

Figure 5.7. Pole Jungles.

☆ *Safety Tip: Action must stop if poles get knocked down. Once someone plants the poles again, action can resume.*

☆ GIVE ME

Skills: *all except poling*
Techniques: all
Terrain: *flat or downhill*
Age: *middle childhood, adolescence*

The instructor chooses two or more teams by splitting up skiers who have similarities: eyeglasses, hair color, eye color, or clothing types and color. These features are the basis for the ''give me'' requests that make up the game. The instructor calls out certain things, and teams must race to perform the tasks. Examples of good ''give me'' requests are partners of two and three holding hands; a person in blue leading a person in red; a person wearing three hats; brown-haired skiers followed by blonds; partners skating, snowplowing, or hopping; everyone wearing his or her jacket backward; or everyone sidestepping.

The instructor establishes a starting line, and players line up as teams, ready to work together when they hear the requests. The instructor also establishes finish lines that each team must race across. I learned to avoid a center point after skiers charged me!

☆ *Safety Tip: If skiers have difficulty with balance or stopping, they take off a ski for better control.*

☆ TRAFFIC PATTERNS

Skills: *all*
Techniques: turning
Terrain: *flat*
Age: *middle childhood, adolescence*

The group stands in a circle, then skiers move directly across the circle to a new location. A momentary traffic jam in the middle forces skiers to veer and turn to reach their new location. As skiers repeat the exercise, they develop strategies for avoiding a traffic jam.

A traffic officer can stand in the center and direct skiers to make quick changes in direction or technique. The traffic officer can develop creative signals (visual or verbal) for various techniques.

☆ *Safety Tip: Skiers may step on each other's skis. The traffic officer keeps directing skiers away from these traffic jams until everyone gets untangled.*

☆ TRAFFIC PATTERNS 2

Skills: *all*
Techniques: *straight run, turns, braking wedges*
Terrain: *hilly*
Age   *middle childhood, adolescence*

A traffic officer or air traffic controller stands at the bottom of the hill and signals to skiers as they descend one at a time. A vertical ski pole means "come straight down"; crossed poles means "stop"; a pole angled to one side means "go that way." The signaller gives each skier several signals on the descent. This exercise is great for developing quick reflexes and changes in plans (Figure 5.8).

Figure 5.8. Traffic Patterns 2.

☆ SQUARE DANCING

Skills: *all except poling*
Techniques: *turns*
Terrain: *flat*
Age: *middle childhood*

Skiers stand in a circle, each stamping one ski and clapping. Anyone who knows square dancing songs can sing along. (I deliberately learned the songs for ski lessons. It's worth it!) The caller gives various directions to skiers: "Pick a partner across the circle, ski toward the partner, swing the partner around, and return to your original location; do-si-do a new partner; allemande left or right."

☆ FREESTYLE SLIDING

Skills: *balance*
Techniques: *straight run*
Terrain: *gently inclining*
Age: *middle childhood, adolescence*

Pairs of skiers get to exhibit their creativity with a chosen theme. The basic task is a straight run with partners but different tasks can spice up the game, like requiring only one ski per skier on the snow, one skier in front of the other, or a 360-degree turn.

This exercise gets the partners talking and skiing a lot to practice their moves for a final show.

> ☆ *Safety Tip: Instructor allows only one performance at a time to avoid collisions.*

☆ FREESTYLE CHARADES

Skills: *all*
Techniques: *straight run, turns*
Terrain: *gently inclining*
Age: *middle childhood, adolescence*

Skiers choose a category: animal, vegetable, machine, famous person, or movie. Pairs of skiers pick a specific item, topic, or person from the category and decide how to represent their choice to the group (Figure 5.9).

Skiers provide plenty of outrageous acting during their descent, while the group tries to guess what the partners are performing. Partners repeat the performance if the group can't guess.

Figure 5.9. Charades.

☆ *Safety Tip:* *If skiers perform by holding onto each other, they have to be prepared to let go and separate before they fall.*

☆ CROSSOVER DODGEBALL

Skills: all
Techniques: all
Terrain: *flat with a square playing field*
Age: *middle childhood, adolescence*

This variation on dodgeball keeps everyone playing the game. The playing field has an imaginary line down the center. Skiers divide into two groups and choose a side for their team. They try to hit the other team members with the ball, and the dodging creates lots of action on the field. People who are hit cross over the line and join the other team. Now they get to try for their old teammates.

☆ *Safety Tip:* *The action can get very intense as skiers dodge the ball. If skiers have poor balance, they take off a ski. The instructor calls time-out if the field gets congested.*

Glossary

Adolescence—Period between 13 and 16 years of age.

All-purpose sports stance—A neutral, balanced stance from which a skier executes all moves; the upper body is upright, the legs and ankles are flexed, and the hands remain in front of the body.

Angulation—The bending of the body along its central axis that allows the legs and torso to lean in different directions.

Alpine skiing—A discipline that involves primarily downhill skiing techniques. The equipment affixes the entire foot to the ski.

Balancing on one ski—One of the most essential skiing skills, in which the skier maintains the all-purpose sports stance over one ski.

Christy—A skidded turning technique in which both skis skid on the same edges at some point in the turn.

Command—A leadership style with which the leader is highly directive and supervises the action closely. The leader is the focus for demonstrations and decisions.

Counterrotation—A difference in pivoting actions between the torso and the legs. The torso turns one way while the legs turn the opposite way.

Diagonal stride—The most common Nordic technique for gliding across flat terrain and up hills. The term refers to the alternate action of arms and legs similar to that found in walking.

Discovery—A leadership style with which a leader guides participants through a series of steps that lead to a desired conclusion. The participants arrive at the conclusion themselves.

Double poling—A technique in which both arms push on the poles simultaneously to provide forward momentum. The upper body follows the arms to provide extra energy.

Edging—A skill in which the bottom corner of a ski digs into the snow. The greater the tilt of the ski, the greater the edging.

Fall line—The imaginary line that follows the greatest angle of the slope.

Free glide side—The ski over which no poling occurs.

Garland—A pattern of turns across a hill that resembles a garland on a Christmas tree. The turns are consecutive and in the same direction.

Gliding herringbone—A technique to slide uphill with skis in a V-shaped position. The skier poles in an alternate fashion. The technique is also called diagonal V.

Herringbone—A technique to step uphill with the skis in a V-shaped position. A half herringbone uses a modified or half-V position.

Kick double pole—Double poling combined with an extra push from the leg; also known as a single-step double pole. The swing of the leg provides more power than double poling alone.

Marathon skate—Double poling combined with an extra push from an angled or skating ski. The technique is used in ski tracks to gain extra power.

Middle childhood—Period between 6 and 12 years of age.

Moving from ski to ski—Transferring weight from one ski to the other one. Complete weight transfer occurs when the skier is able to balance in the all-purpose sports stance over one ski at a time.

Nordic skiing—A discipline that involves cross-country and downhill techniques. The equipment affixes the toe to the ski and leaves the heel free.

Nordic downhill skiing—A blend of Alpine and Nordic skiing techniques; also known as telemarking. The equipment blends metal-edged skis with a three-pin binding.

Parallel turn—A turning technique with which the skis remain parallel or equidistant from each other.

Partnership—An organization that encourages interaction and reciprocal learning between two skiers.

Poling—Planting the poles to increase a skier's momentum or to guide a skier through a turn; a timing device used to aid rhythmic skiing.

Power side—The ski over which poling occurs.

Preschool—The period between 2 and 5 years of age.

Problem solving—A leadership style with which the leader encourages active experimentation by participants, who find numerous solutions to a particular problem.

Pushing off—A Nordic skill that creates good traction and propels a skier forward; also known as gripping because the ski's wax pocket grips the snow to create traction.

Reciprocal—A learning style with which the leader encourages participants to be observers, evaluators, and performers. The leader helps participants perform these roles.

Sideslipping—Skidding the skis to the side and forward down the hill.

Sidestepping—Lifting one ski at a time across the snow to move sideways.

Single-step double pole—Double poling combined with an extra push from the leg; also known as a kick double pole. The swing of the leg provides more power than double poling alone.

Skate turn—A turning technique with which a skier can accelerate around corners using a V-shaped position with the skis. The skier steps off the outside ski and points the inside ski toward the new direction before gliding onto it.

Skating (no poles)—A technique to provide forward momentum; the skis form a V or angled shape. The skier steps off one ski, glides onto the diverging ski, and then glides back to the original ski.

Skidding—A skill in which the skis slip sideways and forward against the snow.

Skill—A simple action or task that is part of a more complex move; proficiency in performing the task.

Small group—Four or five people working together in an independent group.

Steering—Turning the ski with the rotary force of the leg and foot.

Straight run—Sliding downhill in the all-purpose sports stance with the skis parallel.

Task—A leadership style in which the leader challenges participants to perform specific tasks. Participants develop independence from the leader and increase decision-making abilities.

Technique—A combination of skills that creates a more complex movement on snow.

Telemark turn—The oldest turning technique; the skier sinks into a curtsy, and the skis form one long curve to carve the turn. Ski jumpers use a telemark landing because the low position increases stability.

V1—A Nordic skating technique that combines double poling with skating. For every two skating steps the skier poles once. Skiers use the technique on groomed snow with no tracks.

V2—A fast skating technique that combines double poling with skating. For every two skating steps, the skier poles twice. Skiers use the technique on groomed snow with no tracks.

Wedge—A fundamental downhill technique to control speed; the skier angles the skis inward in an A shape and presses them against the snow. This is also known as the snowplow. A braking wedge is wider with the skis edged more aggressively against the snow. A gliding wedge is narrower with the skis flatter to the snow.

Wedge turns—A turn with the skis in an A-shaped position. Linked wedge turns are usually gliding wedges; the narrower width makes it easier to begin and end the turn.

References

Alderson, J. (1981). *Captain Zembo's ski teaching guide for kids*. San Raphael, CA: Professional Ski Instructors of America.

Fluegelman, A. (Ed.) (1976). *New games*. Garden City, NY: Doubleday.

Hall, W. (1985). *Cross-country skiing right*. Lakewood, CO: Professional Ski Instructors of America.

Jerome, J. (1980). *The sweet spot in time*. New York, NY: Avon Books.

Mosston, M. (1966). *Teaching physical education*. Columbus, OH: Charles E. Merrill.

New Games Foundation. (1981). *More new games*. Garden City, NY: Doubleday.

Sjostrom, M. (Ed.) (1987). *Teaching guide for children's instructors*. Latham, NY: Eastern Professional Ski Instructors Association.

Sjostrom, M. (Ed.) (1988a). *Kids in the middle*. Unpublished supplement to *Teaching guide for children's instructors*. Gorham, NH.

Sjostrom, M. (1988b). *Variety is the spice of life—and skiing!* Unpublished supplement to *Teaching guide for children's instructors*. Gorham, NH.

Suggested Readings

Abraham, H. (1980). *Teaching concepts*. Boulder, CO: Professional Ski Instructors of America.

Abraham, H. (1983). *Skiing right*. Boulder, CO: Johnson Books.

Borowski, L. (1986). *Ski faster, easier*. Champaign, IL: Leisure Press.

Flemmen, A., & Grosvold, O. (1982). *Teaching children to ski*. Champaign, IL: Human Kinetics.

Goodman, J., & Weinstein, M. (1980). *Playfair*. San Luis Obispo, CA: Impact.

Gullion, L. (1986). *Cross-country ski instructor's manual*. Northfield, MA: Northfield Mountain Cross-Country Ski Area.

Gullion, L. (1987). *Cross-country ski instructor's manual*. Northfield, MA: Northfield Mountain Cross-Country Ski Area.

O'Leary, H. (1987). *Bold tracks: Skiing for the disabled*. Evergreen, CO: Cordillera Press.

Orlick, T. (1978). *The cooperative sports & games book: Challenge without competition*. New York, NY: Pantheon Press.

Rohnke, K. (1984). *Silver bullets*. Hamilton, MA: Project Adventure.

Schneider, T. (1976). *Everybody is a winner*. Boston, MA: Little, Brown & Co.

Tidd, J. (1989). Simple steps: Eight exercises to help you get comfortable on skis. *Cross Country Skier's Beginner Guide*. Emmaus, PA: Rodale Press.

Wagnon, J. (1983). *Introduction to modern ski teaching*. Lakewood, CO: Professional Ski Instructors of America.

Yacenda, J. (1987). *High performance skiing*. Champaign, IL: Human Kinetics.

About the Author

Laurie Gullion, one of America's top ski instructors, is an examiner and the East Nordic coordinator of programs for the Professional Ski Instructors of America (PSIA). She is responsible for the instructor training clinics and certification exams in Nordic skiing. When she's not busy with PSIA, Laurie teaches Nordic skiing, canoeing, and orienteering for the Northfield Mountain Visitors Center and is a guide for Outdoor Vacations for Women Over 40. Her journalistic talents include writing the *PSIA Examiners Manual* and publishing magazine articles for *Canoe, Cross-Country Skier,* and *The American Canoeist.*

In her leisure time, Laurie enjoys skiing, whitewater canoeing, and mountain biking.